New Italian Voices

New Italian Voices

Transcultural Writing in Contemporary Italy

Edited & Translated by
Cinzia Sartini Blum
&
Deborah L. Contrada

Italica Press
New York & Bristol
2020

Italica Press Modern Italian Fiction Series

ITALICA PRESS, INC.
99 Wall Street, Suite 650
New York, New York 10005

Library of Congress Cataloging-in-Publication Data

Names: Blum, Cinzia Sartini editor. | Contrada, Deborah, 1950- editor.
Title: New Italian voices : transcultural writing in contemporary Italy / edited by Cinzia Sartini Blum & Deborah Contrada.
Other titles: Transcultural writing in contemporary Italy
Description: New York : Italica Press, Inc., 2019. | Series: Italica Press modern Italian fiction ser | Includes bibliographical references. | Summary: ""New Italian Voices" is an anthology of English translations of short stories, poetry, drama and criticism by immigrant writers living in Italy and writing in Italian"-- Provided by publisher.
Identifiers: LCCN 2019022484 (print) | LCCN 2019022485 (ebook) | ISBN 9781599103754 (hardback) | ISBN 9781599103761 (paperback) | ISBN 9781599103778 (ebook)
Subjects: LCSH: Immigrants' writings, Italian. | Italian literature--21st century. | Italian literature--21st century--Translations into English. | Immigrants--Italy--Literary collections. | Immigrants--Italy.
Classification: LCC PQ4203.5.I55 B87 2013 (print) | LCC PQ4203.5.I55 (ebook) | DDC 858/.9208080935269l2--dc23
LC record available at https://lccn.loc.gov/2019022484
LC ebook record available at https://lccn.loc.gov/2019022485

For a Complete List of Titles in
Italian Literature
Visit our Web Site at:
www.ItalicaPress.com

Contents

About the Editors

Cinzia Sartini Blum is a Professor of Italian at the University of Iowa. She is author of *Rewriting the Journey in Contemporary Italian Literature: Figures of Subjectivity in Progress* (Toronto: University of Toronto Press, 2008), and *The Other Modernism: F. T. Marinetti's Futurist Fiction of Power* (Berkeley: University of California Press, 1996). She edited *Futurism and the Avant-Garde* (special issue of the *South Central Review,* 1996). Other publications include *Contemporary Italian Women Poets: A Bilingual Anthology* (with Lara Trubowitz, New York: Italica Press, 2001), an annotated translation of Carlo Michelstaedter's *Persuasione e rettorica* (with Russell Valentino and David Depew, New Haven: Yale University Press, 2004), and a translation of Susanna Tamaro's *Anima Mundi* (Bloomington, IN: Autumn Hill Books, 2007).

Deborah L. Contrada has retired from the University of Iowa, where she directed the Italian Program for 30 years. Her research interests include Medieval Italian Lyric Poetry, Women's Studies, Italian-American Studies and the Literature of Migration.

Preface

New Italian Voices, edited by Cinzia Sartini Blum and Deborah L. Contrada, is an eclectic and vibrant collection of poetry, short stories, essays, theater, and prose excerpts by twenty authors from fifteen countries writing today in Italy, in Italian. The writers presented in this volume come from India and Syria, from Eastern Europe, North and sub-Saharan Africa, from Latin America, and from Italy. They are accomplished, award-winning authors of growing international acclaim.

Reflecting a variety of transnational experiences and transcultural sensibilities, the anthologized texts exemplify a broad range of literary strategies and themes. Well-represented are the core themes of migration literature: post-colonialism, conflict, diaspora, exile, inclusion and exclusion, memory and nostalgia, prejudices and other obstacles to integration, the struggles of the new generations, hybrid identities, and imagined transformations that foster constructive interactions within and among cultures, histories, and languages. While many anthologies of Italian diasporas have focused on these experiences for Italians living abroad, the authors in this volume question and expand the historically vexed notion of Italianness by using the Italian language as a means of experiencing and contributing to life in Italy itself. They help readers think anew about Italy as the multifaceted society that it has been since ancient times, a mindset that is a precondition for considering foreigners and their descendants an asset, rather than a threat, to *Italianità*.

Italian is an adopted language for most of the authors presented here, and Italian literature offers a new field of creative inspiration onto which they can graft elements of their original cultures. The authors in this collection show nuanced, varied and deep engagement with this Italian literary heritage. Such transcultural perspectives are infusing new life into Italian literature. The writers in New Italian Voices are again turning Italian into a world language whose impact goes beyond Italy's original diasporas.

The idea for creating an anthology of transcultural writing in contemporary Italy arose from recent classes taught at the University of Iowa, where students enthusiastically welcomed the opportunity to become acquainted with the quality and diversity of the new voices that are contributing to the redefinition of Italy's literary and cultural landscape. The following introduction addresses some of the issues involved in this kind of project, beginning with a brief overview of the context in which the anthologized texts are to be placed.

Introduction

Giving Voice: Reflections on Italian Literature in the Age of Migration

Over the past three decades, Italy has become one of the main destinations for the flux of people driven to leave their homelands by the economic, political, and cultural forces of our age, "the age of migration," as Stephen Castles and Mark Miller call it in the title of their seminal work on the subject.[1] The resulting demographic and social changes have been defined by the Italian media, for the most part, in negative terms. Scaremongering headlines paint the picture of an assault on the vulnerable Italian coasts, a mass invasion disassociated from news about the labor market and linked instead to growing concerns about security. In politics, immigration has been handled as an emergency by the government, and a surge of anti-immigrant sentiment has been fueled and exploited by some politicians, with the effect of destabilizing and reconfiguring the electoral landscape.

Excluded and objectified in political, legal, and media narratives, migrants have challenged these discourses with literary narratives.[2] Literature provides a space in which the migrant can

1. Stephen Castles and Mark J. Miller, *The Age of Migration: International Population Movements in the Modern World* (New York: Palgrave Macmillan, 1993).

2. Elena Benelli illustrates this point in her essay on the dialogic process whereby migrant narratives counterbalance the inhospitable rhetoric of the State: "Migration Discourses in Italy," *Conserveries mémorielles* 13 (2013). URL: http://journals.openedition.org/cm/1419. Benelli's argument builds on the seminal study by Graziella Parati, *Migration Italy: The Art of Talking Back in a Destination Culture* (Toronto: University of Toronto Press, 2005). For a recent survey of the historical background and development of this literary field, see also Marie Orton, "The Politics of Changing National Identity: Migration

acquire a voice — a figure of speech commonly used to define the acquisition of a new role. It can be a "writing of the self into public existence": through literature, migrant writers can, as Graziella Parati puts it, "talk back" to the media and the State and initiate a dialogue with the Italian public, thereby contributing to the process of Italy's redefinition of its culture and national identity in the age of migration.[3]

The dialogue has been facilitated by various *associazioni* (non-profit community organizations), which have sought to promote migrant writing through publications, literary contests, and public events such as forums and festivals. Advancing a better understanding of the impact of migratory phenomena is one of the stated goals of these initiatives. The most notable instance is the Associazione interculturale Eks&Tra, originally sponsored by progressive municipal authorities (first in Rimini, then in Mantua), and currently affiliated with the Department of Italian Studies at the University of Bologna.[4] Eks&Tra organized annual literary contests for migrant writers from 1995 to 2007 and has continued to valorize migration literature through various creative, scholarly, and educational initiatives. Almost all of the authors featured in the present anthology began writing in Italian in this context, and some of the texts we have translated appeared for the first time in collections published by Eks&Tra, beginning with *Le voci dell'arcobaleno* (The Voices of the Rainbow, 1995), which included the award winners and finalists of the first edition of the Concorso Eks&Tra per scrittori migranti. The aforementioned

---

Literature in Italy," in *Immigrant and Ethnic-Minority Writers since 1945*, ed. Wiebke Sievers and Sandra Vlasta (Amsterdam: Brill Rodopi, 2018): 288–317.

3. In addition to the aforementioned book by Parati, see the introduction to the anthology edited by Orton and Parati, *Multicultural Literature in Contemporary Italy* (Madison, NJ: Fairleigh Dickinson University Press, 2007), in particular p. 13.

4. Other notable instances include Il Gioco degli Specchi in Trento, La Tenda in Milan, Kel'Lam Onlus in Rome, Sagarana in Lucca, S/Paesati in Trieste, and Voci dal silenzio in Ferrara.

organizations and a growing number of journals have fostered collaborations between critics, migrant writers, and native Italian writers in a variety of settings: award juries, editorial boards, publication projects, and intercultural creative workshops, such as the one co-sponsored by Eks&Tra and the University of Bologna, in which migrant authors serve as resources for aspiring writers, both native and non-native. These collaborations are indicative of a vital connection between migration literature, scholarship, and activism, which is characteristic of the Italian context.[5]

The term *voice* is often used in reference to this body of work. Writers, scholars, and other cultural mediators often speak of *voice* to make the case, implicitly or explicitly, that migrant writings bring onto the page lived experiences that are otherwise ignored, silenced, objectified, marginalized.[6] The ubiquitous vocal trope conveys notions of agency, authenticity, and authority; it carries, therefore, important implications for people who have been ignored as speaking subjects, and who want to participate in social dialogue. But the voice trope can also be viewed as misleading: given the aforementioned connotations of presence, control, and authority, some argue, it crystallizes the widespread notion that writing simply issues from one person, thus obscuring the importance of culture and intertextuality in the production of writing. The countervailing argument is that "the concept

5. See Orton, pp. 293–99, for a discussion of the characteristics of this synergistic relationship and an overview of its outcomes, such as anthologies and databases that include both primary texts and critical studies. A notable instance is the anthology edited by Armando Gnisci, *Nuovo Planetario Italiano: Geografia e antologia della letteratura della migrazione in Italia e in Europa* (Troina (EN): Città aperta, 2006), which unites analytical essays by fifteen scholars with writings of fifty-five writers.

6. The website of the Concorso letterario Lingua Madre, for instance, states that this literary contest aims "to give voice to those who usually do not have a voice, namely foreigners, and particularly foreign women, who in the drama of emigration/immigration are doubly discriminated against" (http://concorsolinguamadre.it/il-concorso/).

of 'voice,' tied as it is to the material body existing in time, is the appropriate lens or metaphor for language as material and historical — language as the stuff with which humans try to reach and affect other humans."[7] Both arguments, we believe, can be heeded by considering the cultural context, and the material conditions of textual production, and by recognizing the ethical, political, and aesthetic values condensed in the voice trope.

There has been a tendency to adopt a simpler approach to the body of work in question, especially in its earlier phase. Migrant literature was initially considered by scholars for its documentary value, as a transparent means of calling attention to the momentous historical and psycho-social implications of the current phenomenon of mass displacement. This approach seemed warranted in the early 1990s, when the new realm of migration literature written in Italian was characterized by autobiographical works including a number of collaborative projects, whereby an Italian linguistic expert supported an immigrant's efforts to overcome the language barrier and convey a personal story of migration in the Italian language.[8] In this context the term *voice* is often used to indicate the autobiographical nature of the text. Even in these early autobiographical texts, however, the question of giving voice is all but simple: the voice trope here raises a crucial question of authority and authorship, in other words, an

---

7. These conflicting positions are thus summed up by Peter Elbow in "Voice in Writing Again: Embracing Contraries," *College English* 70.2 (November 2007): 168–88 (https://works.bepress.com/peter_elbow/23/).

8. These early collaborations, which scholars characterize as written "a quattro mani" (with four hands), include the following, now famous books: Salah Methnani and Mario Fortunato, *Immigrato* (Rome: Theoria, 1990); Pap Khouma, *Io, venditore di elefanti: Una vita per forza fra Dakar, Parigi e Milano,* ed. Oreste Pivetta (Milan: Garzanti, 1990); Mohamed Bouchane, *Chiamatemi Ali,* ed. Carla De Girolamo and Daniele Miccione (Milan: Leonardo, 1990); Nassera Chohra, *Volevo diventare Bianca,* ed. Alessandra Atti di Sarro (Rome: E/O, 1993); and Saidou Moussa Ba and Alessandro Micheletti, *La promessa di Hamadi* (Milan: De Agostini, 1994).

ethically and politically important question of power relations. As various scholars have pointed out, the question arises from the relationship between the Italian linguistic expert and the immigrant protagonist-narrator. The Italian expert acts as a cultural mediator, ostensibly helping with the clarity and readability of the text, and also helping the storyteller make contact with the publishing market; but this role is never transparent: it must be underscored that all collaborations of this sort "imply a power relationship that is part of the work's origin and characterizes the work itself."[9] One needs to keep in mind that the Italian collaborator's input — no matter if the declared role is defined as "editor," "contributor," or "co-author" — is usually not just linguistic, and it is not necessarily required because of an inadequate level of competence in the language adopted by the migrant narrator. In the seminal collaborative autobiography *Io venditore di elefanti* by Pap Khouma (1990), for instance, the Italian collaborator Oreste Pivetta (featured as editor) did not limit himself to transcribing the recordings of Khouma's narrative. His editorial input, by all accounts, inflected the narrative by toning down the oral quality of the text. This leads us to address another facet of the voice prism: the question of literary voice and related questions of style and ethos — literary voice in the sense of *how* a text is composed, rather than in the sense of an author's own unique voice, which may carry ideological implications inconsistent with the relational ethos of this new literary field.

As already mentioned, the first contributions to Italian literature of migration, in the early 1990s, were considered interesting from a sociological perspective but undeserving of literary attention. Since then, this vital field of literary endeavor has greatly expanded, becoming increasingly varied, and yet there has not been much

9. See Caterina Romeo, "Italian Postcolonial Literature," *California Italian Studies* 7.2 (2017): 6 n.14. See also Romeo, "Meccanismi di censura e rapporti di potere nelle autobiografie collaborative," *Between* 5.9 (2015): 1–28.

change in the attitude of the dominant academic and scholarly establishments, which, as Marie Orton puts it, "still consider this production to be second-class — doubtless a reflection of Italy's social discomfort with migration and the attendant issues it raises."[10] There have been, however, noteworthy exceptions and positive developments. In addition to a number of Italianists affiliated with foreign academic institutions, several Italian scholars have offered precious contributions to this new field of study by recognizing not only its sociological but also its literary significance.[11] The juries of Italy's most prestigious literary prizes, drawn from Italy's cultural elite, have also made promising, albeit isolated, gestures towards such recognition. Remarkably, very early on, the Albanian exile Gëzim Hajdari, after winning the award for poetry in the second edition of the Concorso Eks&Tra (1996), went on to be awarded the 1997 Montale Prize for unpublished poetry. And most recently Helena Janeczek (born in Germany to a Jewish-Polish family and living in Italy since the age of nineteen) has been awarded the much-coveted Strega Prize. Also notable is the presence of an Albanian-born newcomer, Elvis Malaj, among the twelve Strega finalists. Writing in support of his nomination of Malaj's work, Luca Formenton — an important figure in the Italian publishing world — salutes the decision of the publisher to propose a new writer "who straddles two identities" as a "fully Italian author."[12] Formenton underscores the significance of

10. Orton, 290.

11. In addition to Armando Gnisci, a true pioneer in this field, scholars that have played a leading role in Italy include Silvia Camilotti, Daniele Comberiati, Lidia Curti, Roberto Derobertis, Alessandra Di Maio, Nora Moll, Caterina Romeo, Franca Sinopoli, and Raffaele Taddeo. For an overview of changing attitudes among Italian literary scholars, see Maria Cristina Mauceri, "I nuovi scrittori italiani: Vent'anni dopo," *El Ghibli* 8.32 (June 2011) (http://archivio.el-ghibli.org/index.php%3Fid=1&issue=08_32§ion=6&index_pos=3.html).

12. See "Elvis Malaj, *Dal tuo terrazzo si vede casa mia,* Racconti Edizioni: Proposto da Luca Formenton" (https://premiostrega.it/PS/elvis-malaj/). The small independent press Racconti Edizioni, devoted to publishing exclusively

this choice (and by extension the choice of the Prize's jury) by placing it in the broader complex context of conflicting political and cultural developments: on the one hand, the political failure to reform Italy's very restrictive citizenship law, based on *jus sanguinis* (rights based on blood ties) as opposed to *jus soli* (birthrights linked to the soil); on the other hand, the success of a growing number of Italian writers and pop singers with foreign-sounding names and the emergence of publishing houses like Edizioni SUI, founded by second-generation Italians. The mission statement of Edizioni SUI is worth mentioning as an indication of the progress made since the first autobiographical projects facilitated by Italian "mediators." As Brahn Tesfay (one of the founders) explains, theirs "is not a publishing house of immigrants for immigrants"; they are "Italians of foreign origins who publish books giving space to a narrative without boundaries" with the goal of bridging different realities in Italy.[13] Accordingly, their publications include works of authors of various origins — Italians of foreign origins and foreigners, as well as native Italians.

In view of such developments, one might argue that the field in question has expanded and evolved to the point that it may no longer be justifiable to speak of a single body of "migrant literature." Categorization has been the subject of much debate.[14] Based on different critical approaches and on the various backgrounds of the authors considered, other labels have been used: Italophone, postmigrant, second-generation, new-generation, diaspora, postcolonial, multicultural, transcultural,

short stories, was launched in 2016 with a selection of foreign authors. It began publishing Italian authors the following year.

13. "Edizioni Sui, quando l'Africa entra nella cultura italiana," *Africa,* May 28, 2016 (https://www.africarivista.it/edizioni-sui-quando-lafrica-entra-nella-cultura-italiana/106006/).

14. For an overview of the debate, see Raffaele Taddeo, "Dalla 'letteratura italiana della migrazione' al movimento poetico della migrazione," *In Verbis* 1 (January-June 2013): 175–86.

and transnational. The most commonly adopted label, however, remains *letteratura migrante* (migrant literature) or *letteratura della migrazione* (literature of migration).[15] It is important to note that some of the authors whose work is thus categorized object to this designation and consider themselves as Italian writers tout court. One common argument against labeling is that both the biographical/cultural backgrounds of the writers and the literary characteristics of the works in question vary too much to be unified in one category. Another argument is that, while being grouped as migrant writers has allowed some writers to gain visibility, it has also relegated them to a niche struggling for critical recognition. Labeling, some scholars acknowledge, establishes "a division between native speakers, who can claim legitimate ownership of physical and linguistic space, and those who are geographically and linguistically displaced."[16] And this division reflects the tendency on the part of Italian-born intellectuals "to downgrade, and therefore marginalize, the texts written by migrants to nonliterary expression of autobiographical or semiautobiographical experiences that have no place in a canonical classification of the narratives that define Italian Literature."[17]

There are, however, also countervailing arguments in support of the critical category "Italian literature of migration." As

15. The expression, most notably, is still used by Armando Gnisci, who created a database for the study of migration literature in Italy in 1997 (at present it includes about 600 writers and 2000 titles). The original name, BASILI, has been changed to BASILI&LIMM: Banca dati degli Scrittori Immigrati in Lingua Italiana e della Letteratura Italiana della Migrazione Mondiale. The home page indicates that the database "comprende scrittrici e scrittori migranti translingui e di nuova generazione" (http://basili-limm.el-ghibli.it). For the history of the database, see Gnisci's "Introduzione alla nuova edizione" (http://basili-limm.el-ghibli.it/intro.html).

16. Margherita Pampinella, "From Marginality to Integration: Appropriation of Space through Sociolinguistic Competence in Laila Wadia's *Amiche per la pelle*," *Forum Italicum* 49.1 (2015): 75.

17. Orton and Parati, 13.

Margherita Pampinella puts it, this categorization, by shifting the focus from the authors to their writings and their place in Italian literature, "intends to group together those texts within Italian literature that share significant thematic features as well as structural features, the most significant of them being the process of cultural hybridization. It is, therefore, useful to explore a space of dialogue and confrontation with the dominant culture."[18] Caterina Romeo also cogently argues in favor of "approaching these literary works as a *corpus* — however heterogeneous it may be — [as a] means to empower the counter-discourse they articulate and to legitimize the counter-histories they narrate."[19]

This argument allows us to draw connections with other recent developments in Italian literature. A similar case was made, in fact, for the category "women's writing," which the critical establishment used to regard as synonymous with writing that is mostly autobiographical in nature and lacking in literary value/interest. While some authors and scholars underscored the risk of marginalizing women writers through labeling, others pointed out the strategic value of situating underestimated writers in a context of "like" writers and the critical usefulness of defining a space of subjectivity, agency, and creativity in which the relationship between cultural margins and mainstream could be productively examined.[20]

The prominent role that women have earned in Italian literature of migration — as illustrated by the selection proposed in this volume — also highlights the thriving intersection of women's

---

18. Pampinella, 75–76.

19. Romeo, "Italian Postcolonial Literature," 4.

20. See, for instance, JoAnn Cannon, "Women Writers and the Canon in Contemporary Italy," in *Italian Women Writers from the Renaissance to the Present: Revising the Canon,* ed. Maria Ornella Marotti (University Park: The Pennsylvania State University Press, 1996), 13–23; and Carol M. Lazzaro-Weis, "From Margins to Mainstream: Some Perspectives on Women and Literature in Italy in the 1980s," in *Contemporary Women Writers in Italy: A Modern Renaissance,* ed. Santo Aricò (Amherst: University of Massachusetts Press, 1990), 197–217.

and migration studies.[21] A vital connection between the two fields can be traced, in particular, by focusing on the aim to "give voice." An aim that motivated feminist literature in the 1970s and 1980s and that continues to inspire prominent women writers such as Dacia Maraini, giving voice arguably also motivates the work of migrant writers and new-generation writers. This quickly evolving, and increasingly complex field of literary production — despite the great variety of biographical backgrounds and creative contributions — appears to emerge from a shared desire to create social awareness and consciousness about experiences that would otherwise remain ignored, misunderstood, marginalized, and exploited. Several writers have acknowledged this desire and embraced the role of intercultural mediator and educator, the role of giving voice to the voiceless through the literary medium as well as other means, including youth outreach in schools, and other forms of social engagement.

The effort to give voice, however, is complicated by a deep tension between the voice claimed by the authors and the voice granted by society, but granted — as one critic puts it — only on condition that they stick to the role of witness.[22] Some authors have addressed this tension by arguing that the editorial market tends

21. This intersection is explored, for instance, in *Roba da donne*, a collection of essays and narrative texts edited by Silvia Camilotti (Rome: Mangrovie Edizioni, 2009). By including an interview with Dacia Maraini, the collection reminds us that the transnational approach to gender issues characteristic of migration literature contributes to an important aspect of contemporary Italian literature: the work of women writers who — like Dacia Maraini and Elena Ferrante, to name the most notable instances — "interweave an imaginary that is profoundly rooted in Italian culture [...] with some of the emergent topics and issues of globalization." See the announcement of the conference "Elena Ferrante in a Global Context" held at Durham University, June 7–8, 2019 (announcement published by Stiliana Milkova on Monday, November 19, 2018; https://networks.h-net.org/node/73374/announcements/3171385/elena-ferrante-global-context-international-conference-durham).

22. See Lucia Quaquarelli, *Narrazione e migrazione* (Milan: Morellini Editore, 2015), 40.

to "cage" authors of non-Italian birth into the confines of "real life" as if, because of their origins, they can only bear witness to their personal experiences or be the transparent vehicle of shared experiences and memories about the Other, for the audience's benefit — a role which would exclude them from the aesthetic domain.[23] One way for scholars to address such concerns is to call attention to literary output by writers labeled as migrant, which does not fit into the thematic parameters that commonly define migration literature. Another way is to argue that the role of witness and cultural mediator does not preclude the exploration of the aesthetic domain, that is to say, the exploration of literary strategies that connect migration literature with mainstream literature, expanding and redefining its domain.

AN ANTHOLOGY OF TRANSCULTURAL WRITING IN CONTEMPORARY ITALY

The principles that inform the compilation of the present anthology reflect both of the aforementioned ways of addressing concerns about reductive approaches. The volume's title indicates that our selection is not thematically focused on migration by invoking the notion of transcultural writing, broadly understood as writing that crosses cultures and acknowledges the mutually transformative power of cultures.[24] Also invoked in the title is the related notion of the transcultural writer, which Arianna Dagnino defines as follows:

23. See, for instance, Igiaba Scego's 2007 article "Ingabbiati nella vita vera" (Caged in real life), published in the online magazine *Nigrizia* (www.nigrizia.it), and Christiana de Caldas Brito's "Letteratura e migrazione," in *El Ghibli* 7.31 (March 2011) (http://archivio.el-ghibli.org/index.php%3Fid=1&issue=07_31§ion=6&index_pos=2.html).

24. See Arianna Dagnino, "Transcultural Literature and Contemporary World Literature(s)," *CLCWeb: Comparative Literature and Culture* 15.5 (2013): 4 (https://doi.org/10.7771/1481-4374.2339).

> We are living in an age of increasing interconnectedness, where political borders and cultural edges tend to blur and growing numbers of people throughout all layers of society are "on the move" across the planet, experiencing the effects of dislocation, deterritorialization, and cross-cultural acculturation (or transculturation). [...] this contemporary scenario is [...] giving birth to growing numbers of culturally mobile writers, whom I call "transcultural writers." That is, imaginative writers who, by choice or because of life circumstances, experience cultural dislocation, follow transnational life patterns, cultivate bilingual or plurilingual proficiency, physically immerse themselves in multiple cultures, geographies, or territories, expose themselves to diversity, and nurture plural, flexible identities.[25]

We sought to anthologize authors who embody a variety of transnational experiences and transcultural sensibilities, and whose works exemplify a broad range of themes and literary strategies. We have included texts of different genres — and in some cases fusing or transcending genres — which deal with the themes that most characterize migration literature: post-colonialism, conflict, diaspora, exile (both as a physical/historical and a spiritual/existential condition), inclusion and exclusion, memory and nostalgia, prejudices and other obstacles to integration, the struggles of the new generations, hybrid identities, and imagined transformations that foster constructive interactions between cultures, histories, and languages. Various other themes, including religion, sport, friendship, maternity, and depression, are also explored, both in relation to the aforementioned topics, and without any overt reference to them. Some texts address discrimination as the result of power asymmetries occurring not only among people of different cultural/national backgrounds, but

25. Dagnino, *Transcultural Writers and Novels in the Age of Global Mobility* (West Lafayette, IN: Purdue University Press, 2015), 1.

also within ostensibly homogeneous social collectives. Another recurrent theme that exceeds the narrowly defined parameters of migration literature is the sensuous, affective, desiring body as the site of abuse and estrangement, but also mending and creatively experiencing the world with others, both human and non-human. The body that nourishes words, composes verses, and translates languages — a polyglot body, to use Hélène Cixous's expression — is prominently featured, particularly in the poetic selections, as a medium for creation and communication. Language likewise emerges as a recurrent focus of concern and reflection, which connects affectively charged questions of interpersonal communication — seemingly transcending any specific time and place — with the politically fraught challenges facing migrant subjects in their relationship with Italian society and culture. The use of hurtful, derogatory words as a means of abuse, rejection, and division, which some texts highlight, is countered, throughout the volume, by the foregrounding of language and writing as a means of communication and connection, and as a home and homeland for migrants and exiles.[26] Accordingly, first-person narrative and direct speech play a prominent role in many texts, and phonetic spelling, grammar, diction, and idiom are used, in some, to convey both different Italian dialects and foreign accents. Linguistic hybridity and polyphony are, in fact, recurrent features of transcultural writing, exemplified in the anthology by plurilingual poems and various other texts that resound with a diversity of voices. The selection, at times within the same piece, also illustrates a variety of linguistic registers

26. As Iain Chambers writes, "for many writers, estranged from their initial cultures as migrants or exiles, writing itself provides a home: the stories they tell offer cohesion for their fragmented identities. In a similar vein, migrants who write in Italian today express the same feeling of urgency and necessity, the same insistence on the value of writing as a bridge between cultures: 'the place where we exchange our experiences, and each of us meets the other,' says Tahar Lamri, an Algerian writer living in Italy." See Iain Chambers and Lidia Curti, "Migrating Modernities in the Mediterranean," *Postcolonial Studies* 11.4 (2008): 387–94.

and tones. The colloquial is mixed with the literary register; the realistic coexists with the fabulous; and irony is deployed to deal with weighty issues, both as a shield of light-heartedness — a means of detachment from painful implications — and as a way of displacing canonical notions and ossified local binaries, presenting familiar realities from new perspectives and inviting the reader to explore connections with new realities.

The effort to challenge established ways of understanding and speaking about both present and past realities is a fundamental characteristic of transcultural literature. A notable instance is the connection between present-time power relations and the colonial past — a recurrent theme in the writings by authors whose personal stories are inextricable from the history of the former Italian colonies. These writers show how today's voices of prejudice and intolerance ring with echoes of fascist and colonialist rhetoric. Their works call attention to a troubled legacy that has been obscured by collective ignorance and apathy. Another striking example is the recurrent focus on the link between recent and old fault lines in Italian society, which is highlighted by the repurposing of dialectal derogatory terms, historically used to mark local and national divisions, to express intolerance against foreign immigrants. Such a link reminds the reader that Italians, in some instances, speak and act as if they were not part of the same nation, while also displaying a nationalist, nativist stance against immigrants, seemingly oblivious to the many differences that already both divide and enrich the Italian people.

The texts anthologized in this volume question and expand the historically vexed notion of Italianness by using the Italian language as a means of experiencing, participating in, communicating about, and contributing to life in Italy. As Romeo argues, they help readers think about Italy as the multifaceted society that it has been since ancient times, a mindset which is a precondition for considering "the presence of foreigners and their descendants an asset, rather than a threat, both socially and culturally"; another precondition, adds Romeo, is for the intellectual elites to frame the output of the new literary voices as part of Italian literature and culture.[27] In fact, as these voices remind us, a rich plurality of linguistic and cultural traditions has always been a vital component of the Italian literary heritage, from the exile Dante, who wrote his foundational contribution to the Italian literary canon in the dialect of his native Florence, to the experimental poet Amelia Rosselli, whose embattled, multilingual verses one critic compares to some of the poems anthologized in this volume.[28]

The selected texts contain various references to the Italian literary heritage. A notable instance is the world-famous classic of children's literature, *Le avventure di Pinocchio* (1883) by the Tuscan writer Collodi (Carlo Lorenzini) — a tale that can be read as a critical allegory of late nineteenth-century Italy, and thus evokes the conflict-fraught project of shaping a shared national identity in the new-born Italy, a country deeply tied to, and divided by, myriad local dialects and customs. Other instances include Giuseppe Ungaretti, a canonical poet whose work is inspired by different cultural traditions, and who is linked to a past of migration, colonialism, and cultural heterogeneity that is often repressed in the Italian collective memory: these references — as some scholars have argued — point to a critical assessment of the only apparent cultural homogeneity of Italy, and establish a connection between the new transcultural literature and the Italian literary canon.[29]

Such connections underscore that a vital cultural tradition is an inclusive one. In fact, some argue that transcultural literature is infusing new life into Italian literature and that migrant writers (the

27. Romeo, "Italian Postcolonial Literature," 34.

28. See Ugo Fracassa, "La poesia di Barbara Serdakowski ovvero Il miraggio dei versi riflessi," introduction to Barbara Serdakowski, *Così nuda* (Rome: Edizioni Ensemble, 2012), 6–8.

29. See, in particular, Manuela Coppola, "'Rented Spaces': Italian Postcolonial Literature," *Social Identities* 17.1 (2011): 122; and Pampinella, 76.

majority of whom do not come from Italy's former colonies) are turning Italian into a world language: "a first, true experiment of world language" because, Italian, for these writers, is not imposed by the colonial past, but rather it is a language that is deeply loved and freely chosen.[30] All of the writers included in this collection show a deep awareness of, and overtly engage with the Italian cultural heritage, even though their relationship with it varies. In the case of Italian-born writers, Italian is a fundamental component of a bicultural or multicultural heritage and a means of exploring its rich legacy, as well as its tensions and contradictions. For most of the anthologized authors, however, Italian is an adopted language — a language chosen as the result of migratory experiences that may involve multiple countries, cultures, and languages — and Italian literature offers a new field of creative inspiration onto which they can graft elements of their original cultures.

As Igiaba Scego cogently argues in an article commenting on Helena Janeczek's Strega award, the linguistic migration of these writers, their choice to write in the language of Dante and Manzoni — canonical fathers of Italian literature — carries both literary and political implications:

> The victory of [Janeczek's] *La ragazza con la Leica* challenges an Italy that is increasingly fearful of anyone who may be erroneously considered different or alien. And it reveals a country that, despite racist and exclusionary decrees, has changed and will continue to change. Because writers like Janeczek have been mixing worlds and opening frontiers, because they are themselves open frontiers, to be crossed thousands of times, far and wide. In a way, the author's victory is also the victory of a world that is not afraid of the future. A world that knows how to intermix because this is ultimately the

30. Laila Wadia, Interview with Lorenzo Mari, March 2, 2016 (http://newitalians.eu/wp-content/uploads/2016/05/Wadia.pdf).

> destiny of people. The victory of her book is something that rejuvenates, and decolonizes Italian literature.

Scego concludes, and we concur, that at a time of political obscurantism, a time when there is no progress in sight over the question of Italy's outdated and restrictive law of citizenship based on *jus sanguinis*, writers who choose to write in Italian can claim full citizenship in Italian literature based on *jus linguae*: that is to say, based on the language they have embraced and the literary tradition to which they are contributing.[31]

A Note on the Challenges and Rewards of Translation

Translating a series of texts that differ from one another in terms of genre, style, register, and tone, and in some cases are, even within themselves, culturally and linguistically hybrid, posed great challenges. The greatest challenges, for us, were to avoid leveling these differences and to render the full complexity of meanings as culturally contexted. It was in order to convey as much as possible of the original polyphonic wealth and to allow for complex linguistic and extralinguistic realities to be part of the meaning making, that we opted to leave dialect and foreign expressions in the text, and to rely on the paratextual apparatus for translation and contextual information.

The intended result is a new polyphony created by a complex process of intercultural mediation[32] involving speakers of various

31. Igiaba Scego, "La vittoria di Helena Janeczek allo Strega va oltre la letteratura," *Internazionale* July 6, 2018 (https://www.internazionale.it/opinione/igiaba-scego/2018/07/06/helena-janeczek-premio-strega).

32. For an overview of recent approaches to the question of translation as intercultural mediation, see Anthony J. Liddicoat's introduction to *Perspectives: Studies in Translation Theory and Practice* 24.3 (2016): 347–53.

languages: the two translators — a native Italian and an Italian-American — who sought to bring languages and cultures together through collaborative interpretation, as well as the authors who contributed to making this project a truly interpersonal activity. As the cliché goes, something is always, inevitably lost in translation. We hope, however, that the authors' voices were not lost in translation. By author's voices we mean modes of writing that reflect pluralistic, self-reflective, inter-subjective ways of understanding and relating to the world.[33] Collectively, they convey the message that linguistic and cultural differences do not necessarily preclude and may, on the contrary, enrich understanding. To amplify the authors' voices by promoting the discussion of their work transnationally is the main goal of our anthology, a goal we share with other editors and translators who have made transcultural literature in Italian available to non-Italophone audiences over the past few years. Our greatest hope is that this work will contribute to produce cultural encounters through literature, create border-crossing dialogue, share experiences and cultural imaginaries, build connections, and most importantly, increase empathy.

ACKNOWLEDGEMENTS

This volume is the product of a collaborative effort that included all the authors of the translated texts. We are deeply grateful to them for their invaluable contributions. We would also like to acknowledge the University of Iowa students who collaborated on an early version of "Friends for Life" as part of the final project for an Italian literature course: Jose Almendarez, Ross Bittner, Jessica Jensen, Oscar Pachon Torres, Gina Sears, Quinn Veasman, Davide Vigliotti, Taylor Wertheim, Mayela Andreina Zambrano, Wenqi

33. This is the meaning that the terms "polyphonic" and "dialogic" acquire in Mikhail Bakhtin's later theoretical work, in which the term "voice" is used to indicate a point of view on the world.

Zeng, and Kira Zielinski. An early version of "The Tightrope Walker" was published in *Journal of Italian Translation* 12.1 (Spring 2017). We are obliged to the editor for granting permission to include the story in this volume. Finally, we wish to thank the wonderful friends and family members who offered help and support in so many tangible and intangible ways: Azzurra, Claudia, Dianne, Phil, Tom, and all the others who inadvertently found themselves in the middle of this project and patiently replied to our unending queries. And of course, our sincere thanks to our brilliant and meticulous editors, Eileen Gardiner and Ron Musto. We couldn't have done this without you. The mistakes, of course, are ours.

New Italian Voices

Ubah Cristina Ali Farah

Saba's Line[1]

"When I was born I received a brass jar as a gift." This is the beginning of Saba Anglana's story, in which the songwriter talks about the origins of the project that led to the creation of her first music album.

The journey *begins* with her birth: Saba, daughter of an Ethiopian mother and an Italian father, comes into the world in a wary Mogadishu, welcomed by the hands of her grandmother, the *cradle of her universe,* who is assisting her laboring daughter, speechless from pain. Complaining is unbecoming a woman, and grandma, mother of eight and midwife at the Di Martino Hospital, can well attest to that. A brass amphora, then, the shape of the female body, symbol of fecundity and harvest. As the little girl grows up, the jar is gradually filled with sounds: the hypnotic voice of Quranic chants, the hybridized languages of her grandparents of Ethiopian descent deported to Somalia during colonial times, her father's Italian, the lapping waves on the shores of Jesira and Alula, and the voices of the *jiinni,* demons hidden in rusty wrecks or among the rocks released by the low tide, who distract her by calling her name. Saba knows she must not turn around lest she lose her soul.

The road, or rather the crossroads, is the place of temptation. In Italy, that's where little Madonnas decked in flowers often reside, so that they may show us the right path. In literature there are numerous examples of the devil being invoked near the crossroads.

1. Ubah Cristina Ali Farah, "La linea di Saba," *Combonifem,* January 1, 2008. This and the following pieces by Ali Farah are selections from her monthly column called "Frontiere di voci."

For Saba the meaning of *Jidka, The Line,* but also *the road* in Somali, is anything but negative. It's the *white line* (the title track of her album), it's the joining of boundaries, the horizon where sea and sky touch, light and darkness mix, men and women recognize each other and dance in a vortex that unites everybody because it highlights everybody. It's the *possible road,* the way of overcoming the divisions into which war plunged Somalia. "I envisioned writing a piece about the line I have on my belly. You see, this line, up to the breastbone, perfectly divides my abdomen into two parts: one lighter, the other darker. A visible metaphor for my roots," Saba wrote a few months ago. If the jar represents the feminine universal, the grooved belly is its most natural incarnation.

In the Seventies, the conflict between Somalia and Ethiopia and an atmosphere of growing suspicion towards the *enemies* culminate in Mohamed Siad Barre's ultimatum to Saba's parents, forced to leave the country with their two daughters, within forty-eight hours. It's a frantic race, in a feverish attempt to collect, in the shortest time, fragments of life, relics of a past that will never return. Saba is a five-year old girl, dealing with the urgencies of *today* (the *manta* that sounds like a bell chime in the homonymous song, a hymn to the imminent present, for the sake of which all past and future heartache is to be forgotten) — a child forced to rapidly forge a *language* suitable to designating the new context into which she finds herself catapulted. The jar continues to weigh on her fragile spine.

But the paralysis induced by the excessive load is coupled with an awareness of the value of her burden. The linchpin will come from her mother: her jar is like an amphora full of water that will allow her to quench her thirst better and longer.

The only viable path, then, appears to be that of finally *decanting* its content, the maternal language with which Saba's voice is kneaded, the primordial babble that is at once soul and raw material of artistry. Saba wants to be authentic, and she can be so only by evoking that voice buried in her childhood, made up of lullabies, nursery rhymes, and the cosmopolitan language of Mogadishu, a mix of Somali, Arabic, Italian, and even Amharic.

Her intent is to debunk: against established patterns and pure languages, Saba offers us the voice of her spirit, a voice transformed by her will and by the *road* she has travelled thus far.

Katya's Cry[2]

Mama Africa is the travelogue of Maria Rosa Cutrufelli's journey into an Angola traversed by war and engaged in strengthening its newly achieved autonomy. *Mama Africa,* the same title as a poem by Deodolinda Rodriguez, poet and guerrilla fighter, founder of the Organization of Angolan Women. "Africa / Mama Africa / You carried me in your womb / I was born under the colonial typhoon / I suckled milk from your heart / I grew up / Atrophied but I grew up." *Mama,* like breast in Portuguese, but also the endearing term for *mãe,* mother.

Cutrufelli's work is indeed the literary account of a journey, but it is most of all, the story of the author's disillusionment, which unfolded during a historical period driven by strong ideologies.

We interpret the world with cultural tools forged in the course of our lives, tools that are as relative as our single life experiences. Identity, understood as equality, and especially as uniqueness, must be constructed through a constant dialogue with others. Knowing our own boundaries means seeing ourselves reflected in the eyes we encounter, getting out of our own "skin" in order to be, at long last, authentic. As the Angolan poet Ana Paula Tavares says in *Identità,* "Those who are buried / wearing only their own skin / don't rest / they wander the path."

Cutrufelli's diary begins in March 1975, a month before the birth of Katya, an Angolan student I interviewed a while ago at the Giovanni XXIII Center for African Students. Katya's story begins this way: "I am from southern Angola, my hometown is Lubango. I was born on April 6, 1975, and when I was four I was left alone with my father because of the war, the war in Angola that went on for more than twenty-eight years."

And it is precisely the maddening wait for a journey to the Huilà region, from which both Katya and Tavares hail, that will

2. Ali Farah, "Il grido di Katya," *Combonifem,* February 1, 2008.

lead Cutrufelli to abdicate once and for all. It is July 1976, they keep telling her it will soon be possible to visit the south: "everyone rolls out time in front of me as if it were a magic carpet with the power to get me into a foreign yet friendly world the conquering of which requires patience, optimism. And yes, time."

Three years later, in April 1979, Katya's family is split in half while traveling on a train. "At that age, you know that children are never afraid, so I just watched and saw my mother move farther and farther away, with my brothers, but I didn't cry." This is the final memory of a separation that will last for eighteen years. Katya is the youngest child, the fourth after three brothers.

"Mom wasn't able to come back, barriers were very strong. If you are on the side of the guerrillas, you don't know how long you'll survive, nor when you'll be reunited with your family. We were on the government side, in the city, and they were under guerrilla control."

The first news reaches her eleven years later thanks to the mediation of the Red Cross. But wartime means a long time to wait. "I cherish the memory of a time / without time / before war, / harvests / and ceremonies" (Tavares, *Radici*).

The situation on the side controlled by the government is calmer until 1992, when war explodes in the city, too. It will last ten years. And during a truce, unexpectedly, Katya's mother will finally manage to reach her daughter.

"With so much joy, so much emotion, I know only that I dropped my things, my bag, my coat. I was undressing and didn't realize it, I found myself facing her, I cried, I screamed, I kept saying, 'From now on, I too have a mother.'"

When I interviewed her, Katya was about to graduate with a degree in Economics and dreamed of finally reuniting with her fiancé, who was studying Medicine in Moscow. Together, they would plan their return.

Maimuna's Hands[3]

I arrive at Valmontone late in the afternoon on the train that goes from Rome to Cassino. Almost by chance I discover an art exhibition, as I walk through the rooms undergoing renovation in the Doria Pamphili palace. In the last room, just before the dark, musty one where remnants of the old partition walls are still visible, are Maimuna's white works, densely embroidered fabric sculptures, bodies, busts, and numerous hands. The five fingers, *qamza* in Arabic, are a symbol of the five pillars of Islam. The hand also represents giving and receiving, it's the "imprisoned hand" of those who are forced to bridle their dreams, live beneath their potential. We may be caged by our own prejudices, represented by an aviary full of minuscule human figures or perhaps by a doll in a burka lying next to a generator.

Born in Pakistan, as a child Maimuna attends the schools of the Franciscan nuns. "Embroidery would take many hours of learning" to the detriment of science, deemed unsuitable for the education of Muslim schoolgirls. After graduating from the Brera Fine Arts Academy, she spends a long time painting works in the manner of Matisse, Bonnard, and Picasso. She's not satisfied, feels superficial, and refuses to show her work in public.

"All the women in my sculptures have a red dot on their foreheads and this dot represents unexpressed creativity, the strength we must recognize in ourselves lest it turn into discontent." That little red dot was her latent need, an omen to start reinventing herself by creating her own new and very unique language. Her sudden hair loss is just the subsequent expression of a need that sets a quest in motion, a quest that, after a period of isolation in the countryside near Gubbio, will "reconnect" her to her roots.

3. Ali Farah, "Le mani di Maimuna," *Combonifem,* July 1, 2008.

This marks the beginning of her recovery of the art of embroidery, a form of expression that creates a bond with women of all times, women she seeks to give back a voice because, as Helène Cixous puts it, "we must weave ourselves with the other so that a polyglot body creator of languages may grow."

Many of the sewn works realized by Maimuna are dolls, objects from her granddaughters' childhood or from her own, simulacra, each dedicated "to an oppressed woman, whose story I read in the paper, or I had the opportunity to meet." Hence the little water madonnas attached to a water meter, created after meeting two young Indian women who lived under constant water shortage. And the dreamers, "women like me" who wish to fly, wool flakes hanging by a wire that represents their precariousness and temerity.

The curator of Rome's Galleria 126, entirely devoted to women, which hosts Maimuna's works, is driven by a spirit that matches the artist's project. "I'm against elitist art," says Federica Di Stefano. "I think art must have a social function. Many times people are afraid of walking into a gallery, they're curious, but feel inadequate. It's to facilitate this contact that I always keep the doors wide open, even in the dead of winter."

It's a rainy day, and as we walk on the cobblestones Maimuna scans the surroundings in search of material useful for her work. In her handbag she always carries small plastic sacks to collect fragments, details of the real that may contribute to her project.

Crushed cans, Coca-Cola caps, objects of consumerism, as well as religious symbols, such as the Rosa Mystica, or the intact mirror and the wool sacred to the Sufis, but especially fabrics are her favorite "materials." "Textiles preserve the moods and memories of those who owned them."

Reclaiming objects means filling them with meaning, and creating symbols with a new significance through which we may reconnect with the sacredness of life.

Tiziana's Rage[4]

"I went down this road and people wouldn't give me the time of day but now Quinse blows all the other misses away."[5]

I am at Rome Termini Train Station. It's almost sunset. At last, I see Miss Quinse/Tiziana in person. The only female Afro-Italian rapper I've heard about, she has a powerful, deep voice and her rhymes speak of self-esteem (or *self-celebration,* as she calls it) yet to be cultivated. I have been looking for her for a long time, first on My Space, intrigued by the raves of a mutual friend, then from lead to lead, until I got to her musician father, Adão Ramos. She's wearing a pink top, loose-fitting Bermuda shorts, and on her wrists, the black rubber gaskets she's so fond of.

She finds her musical vocation early: "My father was one of my favorite artists. I used to listen to his music all the time." When she is about sixteen, she discovers rap. Adão Ramos, composer of traditional Cape Verdian music, doesn't approve and doesn't understand her attachment to her own group. "One of the biggest fights with my father is that he wants me to be a solo artist, but we are a family, my group and I, we've grown up together." Last year, Tiziana gets the opportunity to collaborate with her father, write lyrics for him, teach him how to record, and for the first time her father listens to her approvingly.

She has her first experiences with the groups *DHA paura* and *I soliti sospetti* from Anzio, from whom she parts because of personal differences. It will be a trip to São Nicolau, on her parents' island, that will change her frame of mind: "I'm reborn every time I'm

4. Ali Farah, "La rabbia di Tiziana," *Combonifem,* September 1, 2008.

5. All of the quoted lyrics are translated from the song "Senza fiato," in the 2005 album *Kill Phil* (https://genius.com/Miss-quinse-senza-fiato-lyrics; https://www.youtube.com/watch?v=ItvtSw9qvDY).

there. I found peace of mind, and so I returned to Rome with the idea of starting all over again."

Tiziana wore an electric-blue t-shirt with the number 15 she got from the DJ of her old group — she still treasures this t-shirt, now threadbare — and there were some kids calling her, Quinze, Quinze! "I wanted to start over with the spirit and sunny disposition I picked up down in Cape Verde, and so I thought, since I've such a strong connection with my country, I'll take this new name."

"Rapping is my passion and sometimes is for venting / the best way of releasing this fire of white-hot rage / that turns into a blaze."

When she is a child her parents speak to her in Italian because they fear that she may mix up languages, but they communicate intensely in Cape Verdean with each other and with their friends. "In school I was around my Italian classmates because I was the only black kid in the entire school, and I spent the weekends around people from my country." Rap helps Tiziana escape from silence, offering an outlet for the rage she holds in. The school years are very difficult for her, and her performance suffers from it: "The boys teased me a lot, but I beat the crap out of them! There was one day when I said to my mother, "Mom, why am I black? Couldn't I have been born white?""

"It's fair, right? Here in Italy is where I was born / but I've got no citizenship according to Rome."

Being denied citizenship is the real breaking point for her: "At age eighteen I was just like any other non-EU immigrant. I mean, they didn't take into account that I was born here, I studied here, I did everything here, I wasn't studying at the time, I was working, but off the books, so my income was ineligible according to the Bossi-Fini Law."[6] As a result of this situation, she gets a fever in

6. The Bossi-Fini Law (passed August 26, 2002) is named after Umberto Bossi (leader of the Northern League) and Giancarlo Fini (leader of the post-fascist party Alleanza Nazionale), the sponsors of a zero-tolerance immigration bill.

the middle of summer, falls into a deep depression, and emerges from it only with the help of a "somewhat curious" lady, who traveled and "read up on Buddhism." "She made me talk for three months straight. It was better than seeing a psychologist, but she wouldn't tell me what I should do, she gave me phrases to ponder on." From her, she comes to understand that people are different from one another and learns also to be less angry.

Miss Quinse dreams of "hitting it big," first of all so she can tell her mother to quit working, and certainly to help Cape Verde because "money, of course, is useful, but it's only material stuff." People in Cape Verde are happier: "maybe there they still do this thing where they have a good time with very little, that's why they get lost when they see Western countries, because they see all that they don't have and start chasing after it."

"I've got no easy life, but no laments / I've got my mother, the I.S.I.,[7] and I'm content."

7. I.S.I. stands for the Roman hip hop group *I soliti ignoti* (the usual unknowns).

Clementina Sandra Ammendola

What They Say about Me[1]

They say that I'm rather dumb and that I'm not proud of myself. They say that when I walk I swish my tail just to scare or chase off flies. They say that all I can do is moo, that I'm a ruminant, and that I have two horns and four stomachs.

What they say about me.

They say that cows fall into two categories: useful and sacred. Useful cows provide milk, leather, and steaks. Sacred cows are part of some peoples' religion and can't be eaten. If you ask me, we cows are the most important animals in the world. And we've always had to migrate, leaving our own land.

What they say about me.

They say — some German scientists have recently discovered this — that cows can tell which way is north: they head north, sleep and eat facing north, and don't get lost. Scientists don't quite know how we cows learned to find our bearings. They say that we are or we have a compass, perhaps an inner compass that always takes us somewhere else.

What they say about me.

They say that there are sacred cows and that they have always existed. And for ancient peoples, respectful of the laws of the gods, cows are a gift precisely from their gods and can't be eaten, and

1. The story "Si dice di me," written by Clementina Sandra Ammendola and illustrated by Gabriela Rodriguez Cometta, won the 2009 Migrant Literature for Children Award "Sono partito dall'altra parte del libro per incontrarti." It has been published in the homonymous volume (Rome: Sinnos, 2009).

those who mistreat them go to jail. Sacred cows are luckier than useful ones. Today in India they still wander freely in the streets and people make way for them.

What they say about me.

They say that there are minor cattle breeds of foreign origin: like the African Longhorn. And it's hard to understand. They are very docile animals with the largest horns in the world. Their horns can span more than eight feet. And it's hard to understand why they're not declared part of the Heritage of Humanity. That way they wouldn't be just circus animals or a name in the Guinness Book of Records or, worse yet, be hunted for their very horns.

What they say about me.

They say that the most famous useful cow is the Dutch cow. She is a cow that has migrated to many countries because she's very stocky and produces an incredible amount of milk, up to eight thousand liters over the three-hundred-day milking period. One might say she is very generous.

What they say about me.

They say that the useful cows have "the godmother," the one who leads and guides the others. The others are called "ordinary," which is in fact what they are, and they must follow the godmother who has a bell attached to her neck. And they follow the bell cow so they don't get lost and end up alone.

What they say about me.

They say that a big and beautiful cow can win awards. They have shows at fairs, and a cow that belongs to a certain breed, the best of breed, gets the award. Breeds intermingle. They also say that I am the best in the world since I come from Argentina.

They say I am the best because in the Pampas — an immense expanse of plains — there are many cows of many breeds, and we all have lots of space to graze, and we eat clover and fresh grass, they say, and our milk and our meat become better. But I don't know that I'm the best, quite the contrary. I think that we are all quite similar and that in life we just have more or less good fortune.

With cows you can make a milk dessert, milk caramel[2] to be clear, the best dessert in the world, according to the Argentinians. All Argentinians, boys and girls of all ages, and all adults, are capable of eating spoonful after spoonful of milk caramel, and in no time it's all gone. You might say they devour it, because they like it so much. They say that each Argentinian consumes about three kilos of milk caramel per year.

Where I'm from, in Argentina, there's a story that many, many years ago, in 1930 I believe, a cow showed up at school in Quebrada de Humahuaca, in the northern part of the country. The teacher was scared and didn't want her in the classroom. The children laughed and laughed so much that no one studied any more. People in the neighborhood came by bicycle, on horseback, and on foot to see the studious cow, for that's what they called her. The studious cow was brave and pondered over the lessons and learned all of her letters. And Maria Elena, an Argentinian poet, wrote a song for her.

The studious and brave cow was able to migrate to the Pampas of Buenos Aires. And that's how she met a bull from Italy, from Piedmont, born right in Turin, and the cow and the bull started a family, as they say.

The studious and brave cow became godmother to the ordinary cows and, while they were grazing, she told many stories that she had read in school. Then she pondered with them about the Italian land of her bull and how homesick the bull was because he had become old and could never return to his homeland.

2. Also known as *dulce de leche.*

Then a few ordinary cows decided to go to school and later felt the strong urge to migrate, and they reached the largest river in Argentina, the Río de la Plata, in search of a ship.

With the ship, and a bit of fear, we managed to cross the Ocean and arrived at the Port of Genoa. Then, with great excitement, we arrived at our grandfather's land, right here in Turin. And we started grazing and making lots of milk, lots of leather, and lots of steaks.

What they say about me.

They say that when a cow goes to school she is no longer the same and will be, in a way, always a migrant. With letters, the letters that make up many books, one can open worlds and cross many borders and write stories. And I am happy that my grandmother, I mean the studious and brave cow, went to school. Otherwise I wouldn't be able to write, like this, everything they say about me.

Paul Bakolo Ngoi

Half a Lesson[1]

Buyamba, known as Buio or Dark, not only for his tar-colored skin but also for his way of always being sullen and reserved, had decided to go to the soccer stadium for the first time. He hadn't had the chance to go to a game since he'd been in Italy. A big fan of his national team and of the Daring Faucon of Kinshasa,[2] better known as "Imana matiti mabe," he couldn't understand why he had waited so long to go to the stadium. Maybe because he didn't yet have the hang of the land that had taken him in. Certainly this, his first time, would be a positive thing. He wanted to go to the stadium to watch the game, not to root for a team — less emotional involvement, no brawls, and above all, he'd enjoy the show, watching not only the players on the field but also the fans of the opposing sides.

A chance to begin to understand something more about that city with its muggy heat in the summer months and a cloak of fog covering it in the winter. Despite their complaints, the local people were used to living like that, the heat and the fog were viewed like relatives or maybe even like brothers who are annoying, but are part of the family. Without them, the city, the family, wouldn't be the same. Poets and singers wrote verses about those two characteristic moments in time of the city. Buyamba thought of all this as he headed to the stadium on foot.

---

1. Paul Bakolo Ngoi, "Una lezione a metà," in *Destini sospesi di volti in cammino,* ed. Roberta Sangiorgi and Alessandro Ramberti (Santarcangelo di Romagna (RI): Fara Editore, 1998).

2. Capital and largest city of the Democratic Republic of the Congo (formerly Zaire).

Like him, other people were going in the same direction. Unlike him, they carried home team banners, scarves, and megaphones. An unbelievably crowded bus passed near him and was bombarded with whistles and insults of all kinds. As the bus passed, a chorus arose, a kind of patriotic chant in favor of the home team with a lot of cursing aimed at the fans of the opposing team. Buio greatly enjoyed the spectacle. For a few moments his thoughts flew to the heated games between Vita Club and Imana, or between Bilima and Imana, the three most popular teams of his country. He would have liked to sing "Imana matiti mabe, banga Imana," the song that united the fans of his club and that was so dear to all the supporters of his beloved team. He heard a car horn honk behind him and the driver passing two millimeters from him yelled "Blackie!"[3]

Buio didn't even have time to realize what was happening before a group of kids near him were throwing all sorts of stuff at that Renault. When the driver saw the furious group, he chose to burn rubber, barely escaping with his life, rather than ask why so much rage was directed at him.

---

3. Until the 1970s, the Italian words *negro, nero* and *di colore* (in English *negro/ blackie*, *black* and *of color)* were generally used as synonyms, all with similar semantic connotations, although the latter two words were used primarily as adjectives. When "Black" replaced the negatively charged English word "Negro" in America in the 70s, translators also began to disallow its ostensible Italian equivalent "negro," in favor of "nero." By the 1990s the notion of political correctness, another American export, began raising complicated issues of language sensitivity for Italian as well. Italy's arbiter of the Italian Language, the *Accademia della Crusca*, acknowledges that the use of "negro" is now problematic and that both "nero" and "di colore" are not without controversy as well. They suggest that the wise course is to avoid overt references to skin color of any kind when it serves no useful purpose. In the real world, of course, as the stories in this anthology testify, these derogatory terms are still very much a part of the Italian linguistic landscape: sometimes they are deliberately used to offend, at other times the usage may seem almost affectionate to the speaker (but not necessarily to the person on the receiving end of the remark). The choice of how to render "negro" in these texts is unique to each selection. Sometimes the authors have specified a vocabulary choice; in other cases, we have done our best to leave the authors' messages unchanged, while attempting to respect the semantic sensitivities of all.

"This will teach him a lesson, friend," said a pleasant looking and well-dressed young man.

"But..."

"You have nothing to fear. We don't like certain things. We'd have defended anyone else who'd been insulted by that obnoxious jerk, just like we defended you!"

"I don't know how to thank you. I owe you one. I'm Buyamba. I've been living in the city a few months."

Introductions were quickly taken care of.

"Excuse us," said Dado, the most talkative of the group, "but we have to run, the game's starting soon, and we're a bit late. Let's hope our team wins today! Don't take it to heart, friend, and remember, 'there's one born every minute'[4]!"

The guys were gone before he had time to thank them. Buyamba hadn't really grasped the meaning of Dado's last sentence, and the words of thanks he would have liked to say to him remained in his throat, while his heart was suddenly full of joy.

Before heading toward the ticket booth Buyamba stopped to think about what had happened to him. That episode had let him forget for a moment the difficulties of living in the city, the aloofness of the people, the housing problems, and his homesickness for his native land. What had struck him was the reaction of those kids to something that he himself had not completely understood, and he wondered, "But is 'Blackie' an insult, or something that reminds you who of you are? Is it a harmless word, or is it worse than telling you to go to hell? Are Blackie, Black, African, Moroccan, *vu cumprà*,[5] all insults then? Isn't there anything friendly in these words? Maybe it depends on who says it, how he says it, or why he says it. I've never seen anyone

4. The Italian saying is "La madre degli stupidi è sempre incinta" (The idiots' mother is always pregnant).

5. A derogatory term for street vendors of African origin.

at the coffee shop get angry when Giorgio says 'Hi, Blackie!' to me. Maybe it's because he's the only friend I have in this city, and he's the one who gives me advice and really helps me."

Lost in his own thoughts, Buyamba had forgotten about the game for a moment. Words like friendship, solidarity, respect, and racism had placed it on the back burner. The gesture of those guys meant a lot to him. He would have liked to thank them in some way, but he realized that now wasn't the time. Their standing up for him had been spontaneous. They didn't have time to waste. They were there to support their team. The fact that they defended him from someone's insults was just an unexpected incident. Nothing should disturb their Sunday worship, and not by chance — once the introductions were over, even though Buyamba would have liked to chat — the guys had once again taken up the chorus of cheers for the home team which he knew nothing about. Suddenly putting his hands in his pockets he remembered he had a newspaper clipping with him that talked about that day's game. "Three Points to Get out of the Hole" was the title of the article. It was a long feature that described the poor run of results, the coach who risked being sacked, some players who, according to undenied locker room gossip, had to prove they were good enough for the team, and the president of the club, ready to leave if there wasn't a comeback. In an interview, the leader of the fans expressed their support: "We'll be the twelfth man on the field."

Buyamba read the article carefully because he wanted to get a better idea of things before entering the stadium. The names of the players, the coach, the president, and the fan leader all caught his attention. Looking up at the entry gate he noticed that the stadium was called "P. Fortunati."[6] He had walked by that gate more than once, but he had never lingered over that name written in blue letters.

---

6. Pietro Fortunati Stadium in Pavia, dedicated to the president of the Pavia team from 1930 and 1940, is home of the A.C. Pavia soccer team.

Only a few minutes remained before the beginning of the game and by now there was no longer anyone outside. In the distance, he spotted a kid who was running so he wouldn't miss the opening whistle. He was decidedly late, but he'd make it. The police were controlling the situation without too much trouble. It was an apparently tranquil Sunday. According to the papers, defeat could cause serious trouble for the team, and there was the risk of a clash between the two opposing groups of fans. Two parking attendants were keeping an eye on every suspicious movement around the cars. One of them was following the games being played elsewhere with a little radio attached to his ear.

Buyamba, after studying the horizon, presented himself at the gate with his ticket. The ticket collector tore the stub, smiled at him, and wished him a good game. As soon as he was inside the stadium, before climbing the stairs that led to the stands, Buyamba stopped, curious about a heated discussion between two men. At first he thought it was a matter of two fans arguing about soccer, then he realized that it was a real quarrel. But he wasn't able to understand some sentences, and he began to think they weren't Italians. He couldn't clearly make out the two figures that were partly hidden by the ramp of the stairway that passed right over their heads. Buyamba would have liked to understand the reason for the argument, but the language of the two men was beyond him.

"Ti tsè stupid."[7]

"Al parla lu. Gnurant!"

"Sa ghet al curag' perché vegnat no su da Luis?"

"Perché go nient da dimostrat, mi fò quell che vori."

---

7. A dialect of Lombardy: "You're an idiot."
"Look who's talking. Moron!"
"If you have the courage, why don't you come up to face Luis?"
"Because I don't have anything to prove, I do whatever I want."
"Enough already, you've ruined the game for me. I never want to see you again."
"Get lost, you Milanese *baluba*."

"Basta, ta mè ruvina la partida. Da des in avanti ta vori pù ved."

"Va via milanes, baluba."[8]

It was that very last word, *baluba,* the only one in the entire argument that Buyamba was able to understand, that sparked the rage of the other man, first called Milanese, then *baluba*. Coming out of the shadows, the man shot a glare at Buyamba and passed him, almost brushing against him, but without uttering a word. He seemed bitten by who knows what kind of animal. Still in the same language of the argument, he yelled some words that sounded like threats to the other man. Without waiting for a response, he left the stadium, almost knocking a policeman to the ground. Buyamba had never seen anyone so angry. The other man, who must have been about forty, happy at having won the battle, came out from behind the flight of stairs with a victorious smile printed on his lips. From his appearance he was a very sports-loving fan, and the "Bulls" sweats that he wore reinforced this impression. Tall and slender, relaxed and confident, with black, slicked down hair, he held a tennis bag in his hand and had the air of someone who always manages to get his own way. The man approached Buyamba, the only witness to the altercation, and asked him:

"Hey, friend, which way did he go?"

"Who?"

"Don't mess with me. I'm talking about the man in jeans I was arguing with. Have you seen him or not?"

"Of course. He left the stadium and practically bowled over a policeman in the process."

The sportsman broke into laughter and without further ado began climbing the stairs. But suddenly he turned to Buyamba with a triumphant glance and said in a mixture of Italian and that language Buio didn't understand, "That *milanes* is a *baluba*."

8. The Baluba are one of the Bantu peoples of Central Africa. In Lombard dialect the word is used with the derogatory meaning of "boor," "lout," "uncivilized."

In the blink of an eye the man disappeared into the crowd, and in that precise instant, a shout went up in the stadium: goal goal goal. Right afterward, the whole stadium rang with cheers of joy. For Buyamba they were tribal chants, like in Africa: a goal brings high spirits and the soccer game has its own rituals to respect. It's the same the whole world over.

"Too bad," Buyamba said to himself. "I missed the action and I didn't catch the goal. Judging from the comments, it must have been a great goal."

The important thing was that the team had scored and was playing well. In stoppage time before the interval, one of the most criticized players scored a second goal and chants broke out again. It was really a great game, and after the wounds of the past days, the three-point suture that would heal the rift between players, coach, club, and fans was within reach.

The entire stadium was on its feet applauding their favorites, even though the match was still up for grabs since the opposition had come close to scoring on more than one occasion.

The second half opened with a goal for the visitors and before you knew what was happening, the game-tying goal had silenced the whole stadium. For the rest of the game, you could hear some cheers of encouragement here and there, but the spectators had lost all hope. Towards the end of the match, there were only three minutes remaining with perhaps a few more added for stoppage time. When a large part of the audience was abandoning the stadium and the protest was beginning to take shape, Luca Dekin, one of the old guard players, scored the winning goal. A right cross, a stop, a fake that knocked two defensemen off balance, and Luca found himself face to face with the goalie. A left-footed tap in and the player found himself swamped by the hugs of his teammates. A slump-buster goal. A shout rose up from the home end, and for the team it was a return from hell.

The referee signaled the end of the game with the classic triple whistle, and all the players headed to the home end to receive the ovations of the "aficionados." It was also a sign of thanks for their continued support.

"The team was saved in the *cesarina*[9] zone," said a man in the stands.

Buyamba hadn't understood a thing.

"What does Cesarina have to do with it?" he asked someone who was standing near him.

The man looked at him with a mixture of surprise and derision and without replying, left muttering in a language incomprehensible to Buyamba:

"Ma va da via i pè."[10]

While the stadium was slowly emptying and the commotion faded, Buyamba once again began to think about the two men he had seen arguing.

Baluba. This was a word he knew well. But why had the other man gotten so angry? What does *baluba* mean in Italian? He couldn't have been offended by this, could he? Perhaps it was for something that they said to one another before, that I didn't understand.

"How strange life is," the young man thought. "Two Italians are fighting, and one calls the other *baluba* and that one leaves cursing even God. I must have heard wrong. Yes, that must be it — it's not possible that this word could cause so much anger."

---

9. The "Zona Cesarini" is a temporal, rather than physical, location. The expression was inspired by Argentinian-Italian soccer star Renato Cesarini (1906–69) who was famous for scoring in the last minutes of the game. Today "in zona Cesarini" can refer to any event that occurs only seconds before the final deadline. Over time the last name Cesarini has been popularly "regularized" into a feminine adjective agreeing with "zona."

10. "Get out of my way."

So many questions spun around in his head like a pinwheel. To avoid seeming like an idiot he didn't dare stop someone and ask for explanations. "Maybe in the dictionary I'll find the answer," he kept telling himself, and in the meanwhile picked up his pace. Once he got home he quickly jotted in a notebook the three unclear expressions he had to investigate in order to resolve his doubts: a) Blackie, and also "there's one born every minute," b) that Milanese is a *baluba*, c) Cesarina Zone, a new phrase that has little to do with a woman, but a lot to do with soccer.

But it was the episode of the argument and that word that especially tormented Buyamba. That word required an explanation as soon as possible. He couldn't get over that "offensive" word.

"And why *baluba*, if the singular is *muluba*? It's not as if there were lots of them. Huh, maybe he wanted to insult his friend and his whole family. Strange, it's all strange."

Lying on the bed in his room he suddenly felt as offended as the man in the stadium.

"*Baluba* an insult? I can't believe it. What do the Italians know about the *Baluba*? What was that other man trying to say to his friend?"

Buyamba Kalongi Kinda, twenty-two years old, born in Mbuji Mayi, Kasai (formerly Zaire),[11] descendant of the *Baluba* tribe, nephew of Tatù wa balengela, chief of the Luba clan. In short, one who had always bragged about his origins. All his friends knew the story of his glorious family by heart. When he said he was the nephew of a tribal leader, he really meant it, unlike many of his friends who invented stories in order to seem like something they were not. He didn't need to make up tales, his being *Muluba* was reason to be proud. When he could, he never missed a chance to speak in his language, *tshiluba* (or *kiluba*), with some of his friends. He'd missed this lately, and what had happened at the

11. Today Mbuji-Mayi is the provincial capital of Kasai-Oriental (East Kasai), a province of the Democratic Republic of the Congo.

stadium had reawakened his sense of belonging to a people with a glorious history.

In the argument he had overheard he must have missed some elements necessary for understanding. First, he didn't know the language the two men were arguing in, but he was certain of one thing: they were speaking in some sort of pure Italian. Second, he still hadn't understood why one Italian would call another a *baluba,* and finally, what was the connection between Milanese and *baluba*.

Buyamba would have liked to ask someone about these things. Giorgio came to mind, but the coffee shop was closed that day. In his heart he felt wounded, but above all, impotent. He should have asked that man in the stadium for explanations as soon as he had spoken to him, but the fact that they were speaking in a language other than regular Italian had made him think that the guy wouldn't understand.

Buyamba continued to toss and turn in bed, and suddenly he stopped to look at the ceiling. He concentrated on an image painted in the emptiness. His mind had made a trip to his faraway homeland and brought back to him a picture he knew very well.

On the ceiling of his room Operation Nostalgia had begun. Buyamba felt transported to a world he had never left. His old *Muluba* self was back. The entire room was transformed into a large screen where his mind projected images of a return to the past, and never had he felt the need to have someone from his homeland near him the way he did that day. His thoughts flew to his mother, dead a few days after his arrival in Italy, whom he would never be able to see again. Closing his eyes he thought he could hear the sound of her musical voice. He liked his mother's voice so much, and more than once he'd had fun mimicking it. Every time he heard a woman speak he tried to take in the sound of the words that were spoken. This for him was a way to remember his mother. He didn't even have a picture of her, but with his eyes closed, he could have drawn her.

Buyamba was really a strange sort of guy. Often he fixated on little things and wanted to get to the bottom of each of them. The word *baluba* pronounced during an argument had reawakened this side of his character. His being *Muluba* didn't much shape his life. On the contrary, more than once he had skirted past all the obstacles posed by Luba tradition. In short, he was attached to his roots, but lived his modernity without looking over his shoulder too much. He carried his roots within himself and knew very well that at some later point in his life he would never be able to give up certain things. He was convinced that when the time came to choose a wife, he would certainly choose a *Muluba*, as his mother would have wanted. Buyamba was only twenty-two, but he'd grown up in the jungle of Kin-malebo,[12] and for his young age he had seen too many things.

Ever so slowly the sun had set. In the room it began to get dark. Buyamba hadn't realized how much time he had passed in that room thinking.

A musical background suddenly wiped away all his memories, and the image on the ceiling disappeared. Opening his eyes he saw Jean-Jacques Ndeke, a guy from Zaire who had been living in the city for years, the only person he hadn't thought of the entire day.

"How long have you been here?" he asked.

"Long enough to steal this tape."

"What is it?"

"Your favorite African singer Tshala Muana, of course."

"God of my forefathers," exclaimed Buyamba. "Today I'm really haunted by the *Baluba*."

Jean-Jacques, who had put the earphones back on, didn't hear these last words and continued to listen to his music whistling and dancing. Buyamba looked at him and laughed. It was a cheerful performance after the moments of sadness and nostalgia he had

12. Another name for Kinshasa.

just experienced. Jean-Jacques, despite his many years spent in Europe, had lost nothing of his Zaïrian and African self. His way of speaking, of dressing and everything in him was typically "*zaïrois.*" He was a good dancer and sang well too. These were the things Buyamba had noticed right away when he met him.

"Hey, dancing man, stop and listen."

"What?" said Jean-Jacques, still with the earphones on his head.

"If you keep on listening to that song you'll never be able to hear what I have to tell you."

Taking off the earphones and shutting off the Walkman, Jean-Jacques didn't hide his disappointment at the forced interruption.

"I hope you have something interesting to tell me, otherwise tonight I'll strike you with lightening, seeing that it's begun to rain outside."

Buyamba told him about his day. In addition to the soccer matters, Buyamba spoke of the driver, the kids who had thrown everything against that car to defend him, the argument between the two men, the wrath of one of the two, and the strange language they were speaking. He had asked for explanations for everything, but he had forgotten to ask why the word *baluba* was offensive to an Italian, to someone from Milan.

His friend's answers were exhaustive. So Buyamba learned that the two men were arguing in dialect and not in pure Italian, that the guys were die-hard fans and that Dado was a very socially committed young man. Jean-Jacques had explained many things to him, and for the first time they had been able to speak not only of Africa or of Zaire and its problems, but of Italy, the Italians, the city in which they lived, the manner of speaking and acting of a people, of the importance of feeling at home even when you're a foreigner, of pride in one's roots, of friendship and then again of soccer, religion, the importance of good company, of girls. With Jean-Jacques it was almost inevitable to speak of this subject.

Buyamba never had the chance to utter a word. He followed attentively, even if he would have liked to say something. He waited to find a gap to get in the question that had been bothering him since morning.

Jean-Jacques was a friend, but Buyamba considered him almost a big brother because of the five years that separated them. In Africa an older brother is owed respect and when he speaks, heaven help you if you interrupt him. Buyamba grew up with that mentality, and it was unlikely he could have thought otherwise. For a few minutes Jean-Jacques had spoken like a river in flood stage, and realizing he had perhaps stolen too much time from his young friend, he had chosen to end the discussion. Without waiting for a comment from Buyamba he headed toward the door and said,

"Bye, my friend. Don't pay attention to everything I've said to you. Forget it all. Wipe it out. Use your memory for more important things."

"Don't say that even as a joke," replied Buyamba, "You've been a big help to me, and you've kept me company."

"Yeah, like a big brother — just like a real dictator I didn't even give you time to spcak."

"No, not at all. I like to hear you talk."

"Don't make fun of me, brother. I know I'm a pain in the neck, but, once in a while, stop me when you see that I'm going on too much."

"Jean-Jacques, it's OK. I needed to talk to you, and tonight, if you want, we could even go out dancing."

"I like the idea, just give me time to go home and get ready, and I'm back."

"Bye, later, *baluba*."

The magic word had the same effect on Jean-Jacques that it had on the Milanese man at the stadium. The expression on his face changed. For a moment he stopped on the threshold of the door and looking his young friend in the eyes he said affectionately, "Only someone who is stupid, clumsy, and good-for-nothing thinks they see their reflection in another. Be careful what you say, friend."

At these words, Jean-Jacques closed the door, leaving Buyamba speechless once again. During all the time they had spoken, Buyamba had wanted to ask his compatriot the meaning of the word *baluba*, but he'd never found the right moment to do it. Still, he was able to formulate a plan. By calling him *baluba* he hoped to get an answer, and so it was. The cryptic message and the expression on Jean-Jacques' face let him understand all the same that in that word there was no good.

He, Buyamba, member of the tribe of the *Baluba*, would have liked to explain to everyone that being called *baluba* was not at all offensive—on the contrary, it was something to be proud of. He would have liked to run into that Milanese man again and shout in his face that he himself was a *Baluba*. He was even more stunned at Jean-Jacques' reaction, since he more than anyone knew very well the glorious tradition of the *Baluba*. He, the one always lecturing about cultural identity, the value of a person's own origins. Buyamba couldn't believe it.

"I'm a member of the *Baluba* tribe!" shouted Buyamba in his room, "and I'm proud of it."

It was a way of laying claim to his identity and telling everyone there was nothing offensive about that word. His message was for Jean-Jacques, for those two men at the stadium, in short, for all those who dared to see in that word something that in reality was not there.

"Yes, friend, you're right," replied the voice of his conscience, "Nevertheless, never call a Milanese man a *baluba*. It's better not to. You risk ending up with a black eye."

Mihai Mircea Butcovan

In Padania, Dreaming of Mutu[1]

I, being poor, have only my dreams;
I have spread my dreams under your feet;
Tread softly because you tread on my dreams.
William Butler Yeats

"Come to think of it, if they burned down the Gypsy tents tonight, tomorrow we might win the soccer match...Andrei's so strong, but he won't come to school tomorrow if his place burns down too."

That's what I was thinking last night, after eavesdropping on the grown-up conversations my father was having downstairs in the den with his friends. He'd said to me, "Andrea, go to your room because we need to discuss grown-up stuff!" I was already nervous because of the youth soccer tournament match we were supposed to play at school today.

Yesterday afternoon my father had been on the phone for more than two hours. As soon as he put the phone down, it rang again and dad yelled, "*Adünansa,* assembly...we're meeting at my place, before dinner—make sure to get *Giuanin il Viscunt, il Vunsc, Magher, Ratt, Tigher, Diaul, Busciun, Quader, Esercent, tucc!*"[2]

Of all of the nicknames of dad's friends, *Esercent* was the one I liked best. It sounded like the name of an overseas rapper. His friends called my father *Parabula,*[3] maybe because every time he started a speech he said, "*Par esempi,* for example...."

1. Mihai Mircea Butcovan, "In Padania, sognando Mutu," *il manifesto,* January 3, 2008.

2. Lombard dialect: "Jonny the Viscount, Filthy, Slim, Mouse, Tiger, Devil, Cork, Painting, Shopkeeper, everybody."

3. Parabula ("parabola" in Italian) means both "parable" and "parabola."

Mom instead said that they called him that because it was a little like the story of his political commitment. And my mother also used the nickname *Parabula* for my uncle, dad's brother, who's in the union.

Last night they were all there, in the basement den, except for my uncle, and *Giuanin* was saying, "We must send away those *baluba*.[4] Those who rob homes and steal kids and kill people… Gypsies commies baby-eaters…."

My dream is to be a soccer player. And I dream of scoring goals like Mutu. I saw him when I went to San Siro Stadium with my grandfather. Grandpa told me, "We're going to the stadium, Andrea. To watch great soccer and have fun."

Today instead, at school, we were supposed to play against the section B team, super strong. And they've become even stronger since Andrei, "the Rom," arrived. I envy Sergio, I'm not ashamed, and I told him so to his face. Sergio is my childhood friend, my neighbor, and my classmate until last year. Then he changed sections after my father said, at the parents' meeting, that section A had to be for Italians only and no foreign kids were supposed to be included. "And no *terroni*[5] either,…" dad added, through clenched teeth, as he was sitting down. But the other parents heard him, and Sergio's father decided to move his son to another class.

Sergio spends his summer vacation with his grandparents in Palermo. In his class he has one Chinese kid, one Moroccan, two Filipinos, one Romanian, and two "Roma" Gypsies. "The Roma are not Romanian," says Sergio. It was Gabriel, his Romanian classmate, who explained it to him. But Andrei and Sergiu, the two Roma kids, come from Romania. They're great at playing soccer. They come to school every day in a minibus. They live in

4. The Baluba are one of the Bantu peoples of Central Africa. In Lombard dialect the word is used with the derogatory meaning of "boor," "lout," "uncivilized."

5. Pejorative term for southern Italians, which can be translated as "rednecks."

a nomad camp in "temporary tents." They were sent away from the shacks of another camp. "They're a little rowdy, like us," says Sergio. And they are super strong in track and soccer.

Last night downstairs in the den, my father was shouting swear words.

Milan's playing on Sunday, we're going to the game.... Dad uses swear words there too. Last night dad pulled out the T-shirt that says in dialect, Stand strong against the Maghreb South. "You never know," he told mom.

Dad bought that T-shirt a few years ago, at an event where they were all dressed in green, like Martians, or the Irish team. There was a water ritual and everybody was shouting, "Italy out of Padania, Padania out of Italy and Italy out of Europe." Then, with time, they've changed, they still shout, but things like "Gypsies out of Italy, and all the *baluba* back home."[6]

That time, I remember, there was a man with a green bandana who was screaming into a microphone, "We don't want those people here, we're masters of our own house, we're fine by ourselves...." I thought that it's sad to live by yourself. The man with the microphone carried on for an hour. And people got excited, waving their flags whenever he raised his voice, let's say about every two minutes or so. The man with the bandana got

6. The gathering evoked here is a rally of Lega Nord (Northern League), a federation of regional political parties of northern Italy. League members are known for wearing green shirts, hats, and bandanas at rallies. Their official flag is a white field with a green "Sun of the Alps" in the center. Lega Nord began as a separatist movement, proposing "Padania" — a term referring to the Po Valley (Valle Padana) — as a name for an independent state in northern Italy. The ceremonial pouring of water from the Po river (the water ritual mentioned in the story) is a crucial moment of the rallies intended to symbolize the birth of Padania. After transitioning to a federalist agenda, the party has recently assumed more broadly appealing populist, xenophobic positions, so as to capitalize on widespread anti-immigrant sentiments and expand its support beyond the northern regions.

the subjunctive wrong a few times, but I figured it wasn't the right moment to point that out to my father.

Dad was busy shouting, with a green flag wrapped around his neck and his face beet red, "Se-cess-ion, Se-cess-ion, Se-cess-ion."

They were all there, shouting and waving flags: *Giuanin il Viscunt, il Vunsc, Magher, Ratt, Tigher, Diaul, Busciun, Quader, Esercent.* With a rap-like rhythm. "Se-cess-ion, Se-cess-ion, Se-cess-ion." It was the guy with the microphone who had gotten the shouting started again. The guy with the hoarse voice that my father then put on his computer desktop at home. The picture of that guy dressed like Uncle Sam and the saying *"Mì te voeuri!"* I want you!

Every time I started up the PC, I had to face that man, with his tall hat and tailcoat, and his threatening pointed finger: *"Mì te voeuri!"* Worse than the Bogeyman. The Green Man every time the computer is turned on: *"Mì te voeuri…mì te voeuri!"* It had become the screen's nightmare, the monitor's torment. *"Mì te voeuri?"* Somehow the Green Man had taken my father away. In fact, every once in a while, dad would return to our garage at night dressed in overalls, like a house painter, covered in white and green paint. And I would hear him say to mom who was waiting for him with mulled wine, "Awesome *ciulada* on the overpass!"

He meant graffiti on cement walls, like "Free Padania," "Padania for the Padanians," and other slogans heard at the water ritual. My uncle the union man, teasing him, called them "art installations." I don't think they'll ever invite him to the Venice Art Biennial for overpass graffiti like "thievingrome, padaniastate"….

A while ago for my mom's birthday dad had given her an "elegant salt and pepper kitchen set with a silk-screen print of the Sun of the Alps," ordered off the internet. Mom said, "Now even my presents have become party subsidies." And she put his gift in the den for the gatherings of dad's friends. Who at times play *Risik Padan.*[7] And drink "Va' Pensiero"[8] grappa.

Dad says that communism has claimed many victims, and that we shouldn't falsify history. Uncle replies that perhaps it's true, but neither should we forget when we used to go to America.

Dad says that uncle will burn in hell for that "perhaps," and we, however, didn't go "with patches on our behinds." Uncle replies, "Then why do you guys make the Sun-of-the-Alps patch?"

My father sings in the shower, "Va' pensierooo...." And then uncle tells him, *"A furia di lavà el penser...ghe n'è pù...l'è andaa...."*[9] Sometimes mom lets out long sighs and says that those two brothers, sooner or later, will come to blows.

My uncle married a southerner. Dad even calls her *"baluba,"* when my aunt isn't there. "Masculine or feminine, still a *baluba,*" dad told me when I asked him whether my cousin too was a *balubo*. Dad says, "Each in his own home." How sad, each in his own home! And last night, in the den, dad's friends were saying, "Let's organize...let's defend what's ours...brothers on free soil, let's thrash the *baluba*...against the *baluba*...let's unite!" And then they all left together, thanking my mother for the cake. My mother, worried, shook her head.

So if Andrei didn't show up at school for the tournament, we would surely win....

Andrei plays barefoot and is super strong. He dreams of scoring goals like Inzaghi. One day, during break, when Sergio introduced

7. The Padanian version of the strategy board game Risk (Risiko in Italian).

8. "Va' pensiero" is a famous chorus from the opera *Nabucco* by Giuseppe Verdi, also known in English as the "Chorus of the Hebrew Slaves." Lega Nord has adopted it as its official anthem.

9. "Va' pensiero, sull'ali dorate," (Go, thoughts, on golden wings) is the beginning of Verdi's chorus. The uncle's reply, in dialect, plays on the homophony between "va'" ("go") and "lavà" (abbreviation of "lavare," "to wash"): "By dint of washing thoughts...there's none left ...all gone...."

him to me, I told him, "Hi, I'm Andrea, almost like Andrei. But you, if Italy played against Romania, who would you root for?" Andrei answered "Romania," even though they say he's Rom. But he comes from Romania. Then he added, "But in any case, the best should win. And if nobody best, equal is all right too." "Equal?" I asked, because I didn't understand. "Yes, equal, you know, a tie," answered Andrei.

But today at school we didn't play the tournament match. Andrei showed up late to school. Some grown-ups, looking worried, brought him in the minibus, as usual. Our teachers were worried too.

During break Andrei was telling Sergio, "Today I was holding my dad's hand tight…they've burned our tents…we don't know who did it. Dad says it's racist people…'racist' seems bad… if they burn tents where we were supposed to live…maybe they are…my dad was upset, he wanted to say many things to the journalists, but I think he got some words wrong. I'm learning Italian, it's not easy, but dad says to study so I'll have better luck than him in life, and I'll know how to defend myself with words and speak well with journalists."

This is what Andrei was thinking today, on the day of the soccer tournament at school. He came to school anyway and told us that he was sorry about the match, but also sorry because he was hearing people say that they would have to move again, right around Christmas, like a year ago, because people here don't want them. Just when his father had found a job and his mother was glad because they didn't have to go around begging anymore, like a few months ago.

And he told us that last night they were even happy: it was his sister Adela's birthday, the Don, Massimone, had come, with Maria Grazia and many friends, to bring a cake and a doll. It was Adela's first real birthday party. But she said she would probably never be able to collect dolls. They moved too often.

I was sorry to see Andrei so sad. Then he told me, "If you want, we can play soccer together sometime, if we find a place to play. . . ."

Warnings for readers:

Adela, Elena, Elisabeta, Georgia also went to that school, and they were classmates of Adele, Elena, Elisabetta, Giorgia.

The picture of the man dressed like Uncle Sam and pointing his finger *"Mì te voeuri!"* really exists. As does Risik Padan. If you want to know more about Padanian *ciulade,* take a tour online.

Did you have a little trouble distinguishing between Andrea and Andrei, Sergio and Sergiu? That's your business. Did that small difference disturb your reading? That's your business.

That small difference in their names signals many other differences in their lives. But not in their youthful dreams. Which are our business, everybody's business. In fact, they concern us all.

Dedication:

To the kids who kick the *balòn* around in the youth-soccer field of a Milan park.

To the dreamers who gave them the field to play in, the balls, and a few extra dreams.

To those who make children's dreams come true.

Rosana Crispim da Costa

Attendo che il mare[1]

Attendo che il mare
mi dia un segnale
per capire dove arriverò.
Forse, ad un porto sicuro
o in un'isola tutta mia.
Voglio sentire la mia
voce femminile:
sono stanca di fare l'uomo
e derubare con la tenerezza tutte le frontiere del cuore.
Non voglio né un amante, né un marito.
Ma sì, un'anima
per tutta la vita.

Il mio corpo traduce[2]

Il mio corpo traduce
molte lingue,
la comprensione
rimane indietro.
Comunicazione tra marziani.

---

1. *Memorie in valigia,* ed. Roberta Sangiorgi and Alessandro Ramberti (Santarcangelo di Romagna (RI): Fara Editore, 1997).

2. Rosana Crispim da Costa, *Il mio corpo traduce molte lingue* (Santarcangelo di Romagna (RI): Fara Editore, 1998).

I Am Waiting for a Sign

I am waiting for a sign
from the sea
to figure out where I'll end up.
Perhaps, a safe harbor
or an island all my own.
I want to hear
my feminine voice:
I am tired of acting like a man
and using tenderness to rob all of the heart's frontiers.
I don't want a husband, or a lover either.
But I do want a soul
for all my life.

My Body Translates

My body translates
many languages,
comprehension
lags behind.
Communication between extraterrestrials.

Non rinnego la paura[3]

Non rinnego la paura
nascondo il viso tutti i giorni.

La notte è morbida
come il velluto
esorcizzando la pelle.

Messaggio[4]

Si perde tempo a limitare l'emozione,
invece di vivere intensamente
ogni attimo che il cuore batte.
Lui – il cuore – soffre con tanti freni.
Vuole rompere le catene,
viaggiare,
sentire della buona musica,
rilassarsi,
mangiare bene,
guardare un bel film,
ricevere amici,
leggere,
essere liberamente romantico,
vedere più giustizia nel mondo,
crescere,
fare la doccia,
fare l'amore,
essere amato.
Ti lascio le chiavi
delle catene.
Baci.

---

3. Crispim da Costa, *Il mio corpo.*

4. Crispim da Costa, *Il mio corpo.*

I Don't Disavow Fear

I don't disavow fear
I hide my face every day.

The night is soft
like velvet
exorcising my skin.

Message

It's a waste of time to bottle up emotion,
instead of living intensely
every moment our heart beats.
It — the heart — suffers with so many restraints.
It wants to break the chains,
travel,
listen to good music,
relax,
eat well,
watch a good movie,
have friends over,
read,
be unreservedly romantic,
see more justice in the world,
grow,
take a shower,
make love,
be loved.
I'm leaving you the keys
to the chains.
Kisses.

NON SONO QUI PER SCRIVERE ROMANZI[5]

Non sono qui per scrivere romanzi,
i miei tentativi li ho sbagliati tutti.
Sono adepta della poesia del momento,
dell'ispirazione selvaggia,
quella che viene da dentro
senza preavviso,
svegliando bei ricordi
facendomi felice.
Il passato può essere corretto con amore,
soffro di nostalgia e cerco la cura;
compro solo dischi vecchi
i nuovi li lascio invecchiare.
Spero che la musica possa sequestrare
un momento speciale,
radicalmente mio.

QUESTO DESIDERIO DI LIBERTÀ[6]

Questo desiderio di libertà è quasi incomprensibile.
Palpita il cuore al ritmo di "samba-enredo",
e finisce per cadere di stanchezza in un concerto
di musica classica.

---

5. Crispim da Costa, *Il mio corpo.*

6. *Destini sospesi di volti in cammino,* ed. Roberta Sangiorgi and Alessandro Ramberti (Santarcangelo di Romagna (RI): Fara Editore, 1998).

I Am Not Here to Write Novels

I am not here to write novels,
all my attempts have failed
I am skilled in the poetry of the moment,
of wild inspiration,
the kind that comes from within
without warning,
awakening fond memories
making me happy.
The past can be corrected with love,
I suffer from nostalgia and look for a cure;
I only buy old albums
the new ones I let age.
I hope that music can hijack
a special moment,
radically mine.

This Desire for Freedom

This desire for freedom is almost incomprehensible.
My heart beats to the rhythm of a "samba enredo,"
and ends up collapsing from fatigue in a concert
of classical music.

Nell'ombra di una sola candela[7]

Nell'ombra di una sola candela
Danzo con euforia
Così allontano la paura
Di dare mille risposte
Io non mi riconosco
In questo mondo profano
Mi equilibro di sentimenti
Sfidando la mia vertigine
Anche se cado spesso
Continuo lontano da casa
Non lo so dove mettere i quadri
Non ho i muri
Sono un fiore sbocciato
In un deserto infinito
E finché sento questa dolce musica
Che mi resuscita
Proseguirò la storta strada
Della vita
Perché niente è più divino

Dei miei sogni.

---

7. *Destini sospesi.*

In the Shadow of a Single Candle

In the shadow of a single candle
I dance with euphoria
This way I chase away the fear
Of giving a thousand answers
I don't recognize myself
In this profane world
I balance myself with feelings
Defying my vertigo
Despite my frequent falls
I carry on far away from home
I don't know where to hang my paintings
I have no walls
I am a flower blossomed
In an endless desert
And as long as I hear the sweet music
That revives me
I'll continue along the twisted road
Of life
Because nothing is more divine

Than my dreams.

Canzone[8]

Una mattina senza sogni
mi sono alzata nuda —
vestita solo di brezza.
Sono andata a visitare il giardino
che avevo dimenticato:
Aveva fiori che hanno resistito
al mio abbandono.
Ho soccorso rose impoverite
annaffiando con il mio riposo.
Ho visto riflesso nel lago
la donna che non era più una bambina.
Le nuvole si sono unite nascondendo le stelle —
Triste o allegra sono rinata.
Mentre tornavo a casa
sentivo accordi armoniosi,
ho abbracciato il mio desiderio
vicino al camino e
ho cucito i miei tagli,
ricordando i miei amori.
Alla fine dei rammendi,
ha soffiato un vento feroce:
in quella notte sono diventata una canzone.

8. Crispim da Costa, *Desejo* (San Giovanni in Persiceto (BO): Eks&Tra, 2006).

Song

One dreamless morning
I got up naked—
clothed only by the breeze.
I went to visit the garden
that I had forgotten:
It had flowers that survived
my neglect.
I rescued impoverished roses
by watering with my repose.
I saw reflected in the lake
the woman who was no longer a child
Clouds came together hiding the stars —
Sad or happy, I was reborn.
While returning home
I heard harmonious chords,
I embraced my desire
by the fireplace and
stitched up my cuts,
remembering the loves of my life.
When all the mending was done,
a fierce wind raged:
that night I became a song.

Per dirti[9]

Per dirti amore
ho dovuto
vivere mille vite
perché di terra sono fatta
terra lontana e calpestata
terra nostalgica e allontanata
per dirti amore
ho dovuto
graffiare il tuo petto forte
perché di acqua sono fatta
acqua oceanica e sconfinata
acqua salmastra e distratta
per dirti amore
ho dovuto
amare diverse volte
perché di aria sono fatta
aria calda e laboriosa
aria vitale e vittoriosa
per dirti amore
ho dovuto
rinascere senza pentimento
perché di fuoco sono fatta
fuoco ambiguo e seduttore
fuoco amico e protettore
oggi
per dirti amore
non devo fare niente di più
che amarti senza impedimenti
perché di te
io sono fatta

9. Crispim da Costa, *Tra mura di vento* (Patti (ME): Centro Studi Tindari Patti, 2010).

To Speak to You

To speak to you of love
I had to
live a thousand lives
because I'm made of earth
distant, trampled earth
nostalgic and estranged earth
to speak to you of love
I had to
scratch your strong chest
because I'm made of water
boundless, ocean water
briny and distracted
to speak to you of love
I had to
love various times
because I'm made of air
warm, laborious air,
vital and victorious
to speak to you of love
I had to
be reborn without regrets
because I'm made of fire
ambiguous, alluring fire
friendly and protective
today
to speak to you of love
I must do nothing more
than love you without impediment
because I'm made
of you

Sospiri lirici[10]

mio corpo compone
versi cristallini

saliva calda
esplorando i sensi rigidi d'eccitazione
piedi placcati nella terra umida
lingua tra le labbra secche
mani accarezzando il seno del bosco
petto che respira nuvole celesti
ventre in giù concavo e distratto
pupille richiuse nell'abisso dell'immaginario

sospiri lirici
ultima nota
sospiri lirici

10. Crispim da Costa, *Tra mura di vento.*

Lyrical Sighs

my body composes
crystal clear verses

warm saliva
exploring senses rigid with excitement
feet coated in moist earth
tongue between dry lips
hands caressing the bosom of the woods
chest breathing pale blue clouds
prone belly hollowed and distracted
pupils contracted into the abyss of imagination

lyrical sighs
final note
lyrical sighs

Christiana de Caldas Brito

The Tightrope Walker[1]

Only yesterday did I understand how subtle the transition from resentment to hope is. I thought it would be more complicated. It isn't complicated or difficult. It's subtle.

I'd like to tell you how I found that out.

First I have to tell you about the high wire on which I keep myself precariously balanced. Yes, because I'm a tightrope walker, too. I keep away distractions, I avoid memories, and I don't give in to fatigue. But often I get frightened of falling. Below — as I well know — there is no net.

My life? Hours and hours marked by green-yellow-red, with a pail of water and a sponge at an intersection. That's all.

Red. A minute and a half. My body bends over the cars and, without the help of words, it says, "Can I wash your windshield?"

Some accept.

One step forward on the wire.

But right after come those who, with squealing tires, take off in a hurry, as if offended. Or those who look straight ahead and pretend not to hear me. They turn the other way.

I risk losing my balance.

At times I feel useless, like a stoplight when it's out. Cars stop at a distance, and when I get closer, they accelerate and run over

---

1. The short story "L'equilibrista" received a Special Mention-Jury award at the fourth edition of Concorso Eks&Tra and was published in the anthology of selected submissions, *Destini sospesi di volti in cammino* (Santarcangelo di Romagna (RI): Fara Editore, 1998). It is also included in a collection of Christiana de Caldas Brito's short stories, *Qui e là* (Isernia: Cosmo Iannone, 2004).

my smile. Unfortunately there are no laws to protect smiles, nor are there hospitals for broken souls. I remain there, between one green and another, thinking: not even the easy life makes people better. Maybe it's hard to be nice in the middle of traffic. I'm wondering how I would treat myself if I were inside one of these cars. Would I see the wire that I'm now suspended on?

At the very least I'd make a big mess if I were at the steering wheel. The colors of the stoplights have different meanings for someone like me: green means wait, yellow means begin to move, and red, instead, hurry up.

In bed at night I close my eyes and see the colors of the traffic light. I'd like to talk to someone, but my roommates are asleep. I get up to write. But the words, once they are on the page, seem like cars in a traffic jam. They don't go fast as when you're talking. For me the true engine of words is my voice. If I'm talking, my mind is in gear.

And then there are nights when the green light opens the door to nightmares. A spider is building its web. Using barbed wire. It wraps its thread around me. "Dad! Dad!" My father lights up a cigarette and starts smoking. He doesn't run to save me. He just smokes. I'm trapped. Without options. "Dad!" I wake up with a traffic jam in my chest.

If it rains, since my pockets are empty, I can only go to the Termini Station, where the homeless are. They push me and yell, "Go back home! This is our place!"

Why did my father teach me that suffering softens the heart?

Green. Yellow. Red. For hours and hours.

I study the people inside their cars. Some of their gazes pass through my body as if, because of my work, I have turned into glass myself.

Last week I was insistent with a woman. Her Clio was really dirty. She got angry and yelled at me, "NO!" I cleaned her windshield anyway, with energetic movements, pressing hard on the sponge. I let the black water flow on purpose onto the body of the car. I was cleaning one part and dirtying the other.

My rage served to make me understand that I am not made of glass. It confirmed that I have human fabric inside.

But the wire is likely to break, I know.

Full of resentment I wondered, is there any way other than anger to be truly human?

Maybe I could prepare the window washers' manifesto. Very early, before sunrise, I would plaster it on all the cars in Rome. The manifesto would say: "I exist, you exist, we window washers exist. We are not transparent like glass."

Or I could go back to my country. But it would mean walking backwards and maybe even losing my balance when I change directions. Some tightrope walkers have broken their bones. Others have been tempted to hang themselves with the wire.

Green. Yellow.

I keep on washing your windshields, washing your windshields.

When I was a child, I made a building out of cardboard and matches. The windows were tiny pieces of cellophane glued to the matches. I don't know what happened to this silly cylinder of mine, the crystal palace of my childhood. Before coming to Italy, I dreamt that one day I would make real buildings. The trees along the streets would be reflected in their windows. But that was a long time ago. When one could find green not only in stoplights but also in the streets.

Red. "Can I wash your windshield?"

The party, with friends, songs. On the table, the most beautiful tablecloth. My mom hugs me: "Tell us what you do in Italy." Everyone is listening. "I have a cleaning company, mom, that washes the windows of the tallest buildings in the city."

My mom repeats: “Did you hear that? His cleaning company washes the windows of buildings all over Rome.”

Dad watches me with interest: “How many employees do you have?” And he lights his cigarette.

“Forty, dad. Two hundred meters of steel wire hold up our scaffoldings. A real technological web.”

I laugh. But from the other side of the street comes the voice of my buddy who works at the same intersection. “What are you doing, sleeping?”

With a start I place myself in front of a small van. “Right away, done.”

Green. In Italy people say this is the color of hope. But when the light’s green, I ponder. Green today, green tomorrow: the fact is that at the street corner, in front of my stoplight, as a result of not being seen for so long, I have begun to see.

This is how it happened. Yesterday, with the red light a man’s Fiat stopped in the first row. While I was scrubbing off pigeon shit stuck to the windshield, he asked me: “What’s your name?”

Since I’m no longer used to having a name, at first I just stood staring at him like an idiot. I was going to come up with an easy name to avoid confusion — because mine is difficult to understand — but the green suddenly flashed and he drove away.

That’s all that happened. But he asked me my name. I didn’t have time to answer him, but while it was still green I thought about all those who understand my humble and honest effort to keep my balance on the wire, those who call what I do work. And I repeated my name several times, loudly. As if they could hear it.

It’s OK to have a red light that lets you work. But it’s all different if you have a name.

From resentment to hope.

The transition is subtle.

Isn’t this what I was supposed to tell you?

Migrant Snow White[2]

Letter from the Seven Dwarfs to Snow White

The Woods, October 2017

Dear Snow White,

Without you the seven of us are more messed up than ever. In case you're interested, we eat really badly, we fight all the time, and at night, when we get home from the mine, we don't wash up. The house is a complete disaster. Sneezy does nothing but sneeze, and Sleepy has become an insomniac. We had to ask the hunter if he would write this letter, Snow White, because you taught us to sing and dance, but you never taught us to read and write. If you had thought about that, now we would be able to write to you ourselves, without having to ask a person who barely knows us. Our life with you was a fairy tale, but now even the birds don't drop by. Bashful and Dopey cry. Happy stutters. Doc has fallen into a state of depression. Grumpy, crankier than ever, doesn't do anything except hope that your Prince Charming turns back into a frog.

And you, Snow White, with all the space you have in the castle, do you still dance? While you're singing, think of us and sing as loud as you can. If the wind is blowing just right, we'll be able to hear your voice.

Your Seven Dwarfs

---

2. "L'immigrata Biancaneve," a twist on the classic fairy tale, is the unpublished, revised version of "Metamorfosi di un'immigrata nel paese di Ailati," a short story published in *La Bottega del Barbieri,* August 27, 2016. A slightly different version of "Metamorfosi di un'immigrata nel paese di Ailati" had been previously published in *El Ghibli, rivista online di letteratura della migrazione* 3.12 (June 2006).

Letter from Snow White to the Prince

The Castle, October 2017

Dear Charming,

I don't think it's fair that you didn't warn me about the staffing problems at the castle. I used to have seven beds to make, but they were very small beds. Now I have to make a gigantic bed with all those curtains that drape down from the canopy and collect a lot of dust. The silk sheets are too hard to iron. From now on, I will just fold them up and call it a day.

And another thing, why aren't there any apples in the garden? I love apples. The Witch often used to bring them to me. I never regretted eating the poisoned apple. The dwarfs cried, but I fell deeply asleep, and, to tell the truth, Charming, I hadn't slept so well in years. It was your kiss that awakened me. I came with you to the castle, but the very high walls block contact with the woods. I miss my dwarfs. There were seven of them, and we used to sing and dance together. You, Charming, are just one person, and at times — forgive me for saying it — you are a little bit boring. You talk about hunting, and I love animals. When we go on horseback, you always ride ahead, and it's as if I were galloping alone. The books you read are strange, and your visitors aren't much fun. You should be aware that I'm considering the idea of going back home to the dwarfs. Fairy tales can be updated. Don't you think so, Charming?

Snow White

Letter from the Prince to the Witch

The Castle, January 8, 2018

Dear Ms. Witch:

Charming here, the prince who married Snow White after waking her from your spell. My wife and I are in that difficult "happily ever after" period, but something's not right. Snow White is from the woods. It's a different world. Living with some dwarfs who worked all day away from home, she was used to doing things her way around the house. The problem is, she wants to do everything her way here in my castle, too.

Dear Witch, Snow White has expressed the desire to go back to the dwarfs. Could you prepare some apple pies with a spell even more powerful than before?

With sincere thanks,
His Majesty,
Prince Charming

Letter from the Witch to the Prince

The Tower, February 2, 2018

Dear Prince,

I wasted a lot of apples before the spell worked on Snow White. Perhaps it's because she has lived in the woods so long, but your wife has an iron constitution. She must have eaten give or take five or six kilos of apples before she fell into a cataleptic state. But if you feel like tackling this onerous problem — fruit today costs a fortune — I'll be happy to prepare a new spell for your wife.

Best regards,
The Witch

Letter from Snow White to the Witch

The Castle, March 8, 2018

Ms. Witch:

I imagine it was the prince who ordered the delicious apple pies. What can I say? I remember well what happened to me before. I fell for it the first time, but falling for it a second time is a bit much!

I am about to leave the castle. I'll be stopping by just to say hello to the dwarfs and to plan a future literacy course with them. I won't stay with them. I've done a lot of thinking in my solitary moments and my mind is made up. I want to open a grocery store in the woods. I'll teach people to recognize wholesome products. We should all know how to protect ourselves from the dangers of toxins. I'm sorry for you, Ms. Witch, but the ingenuous Snow White of the past is today, on International Women's Day, a mature person who knows how to use her mistakes to better her own life and that of others.

Good-bye,
Snow White[3]

3. Snow White's "metamorphosis" is particularly striking when compared to earlier endings proposed by the author, in which the protagonist eats the apple pie and remains forever a servant to both prince and castle. Here is the last letter as it appears in "Metamorfosi di un'immigrata nel paese di Ailati" published online by *La Bottega del Barbieri,* August 27, 2016 (http://www.labottegadelbarbieri.org/metamorfosi-di-unimmigrata-nel-paese-di-ailati/).

Onthesidelines Castle, March 8

My Dear Charming,

How nice it is to be on the sidelines of Onthesidelines. Our days pass in perfect harmony, dearest Charming, and you cannot imagine how much fun I have standing over the stove inventing new dishes for you. I am moved when I see you greedily finish, in five short minutes, everything I prepare after hours and hours of work in the kitchen. I thank the kiss that made me yours! How lucky awakened women like me are! I am always in motion, I sing and wax the floors of all the various levels of our castle with such joy.... I shudder at the mere thought that I could have remained asleep forever in that crystal coffin.

Since you've been bringing me that delicious apple pie every day — how kind you are, my love! — my happiness knows no bounds. The only thing is, I must be careful not to gain weight. It's OK for you to put on weight, Charming, but I want to be in shape to serve you at my best. I will never tire of admiring your muscles! The seven dwarfs were too short, right? They weren't handsome like you.

If we go on horseback, I like to watch from afar how well you gallop. You are an important man, you travel often, and it's wonderful to await your return. How sweet it is, knowing that we are alone in the castle, without any servants to annoy us, right, Charming?

Kiss me always, love, wake me every morning to make your breakfast! At any hour of the day or night, I'll be ready to do whatever you like.

I love you, Charming!

Your small, ever smaller,
Snow White

Amor Dekhis

Other People's Prayer[1]

If my mother had ever seen me while I was performing ritual Christian gestures at a Mass, she would have lost all reason and probably would have had a heart attack. She never would have imagined that I'd betray the education she gave me, abandon my religion, and possibly convert to another. And given that my mission was only to obtain a degree, she would have just thought that I was insane, because I had never paid any attention to my own prayer, and now instead, I was joining in "other people's prayer."

On the day that I stood up and sat down following the orders of the Christian imam, the decision to imitate those movements was dictated to me, with conviction, by my own contemplation: I was only honoring Mr. Cappelli. After all, the Prophet Mohammed said, "An hour's contemplation is worth more than a thousand years of worship." And I contemplated every day. That was my faith. The fact that I was in another country was an extra reason for contemplation. No justification, however, would stave off the sentence of my mother who, from that moment and forever after, would disown me.

But we were now separated by distance and by time. Since my departure, I had only seen her a few times. At the moment of the other people's prayer, no thoughts of disownment were on my mind.

Determined to find another place to live my life, I had to prepare above all to be open-minded and to be ready to manage

1. Amor Dekhis, "La preghiera degli altri," in *Le voci dell'arcobaleno* (Santarcangelo di Romagna (RI): Fara Editore, 1995).

my studies, and if necessary, a small job, in case the scholarship provided by the state turned out to be insufficient. I had to be aware that sacrifice would comprise a fundamental element of my way of life. Once I reached my destination, the call for a revolution in my mind would translate into concrete acts.

In the weeks before my departure, I was conflicted. On the one hand, I was facing a challenge for the first time and I wasn't sure I'd be able to meet it. Uncertainty caused me some anxiety. On the other hand, a captivating curiosity, an inner drive, gave me courage and pushed me to press forward.

The destination country was Italy, so I made myriad inquiries at the pertinent diplomatic and cultural offices in the capital city of Algiers. In addition to the embassy for bureaucratic reasons, I began to frequent the Institute of Italian Culture. The main activity of this institute consisted in teaching the Italian language at various levels, but I limited myself to leafing through brochures or watching some films that documented the characteristics of the *Bel paese*. I got to know the staff. At the institute I often met the man from the consulate who handled cultural matters and therefore students seeking a visa. He had a Fiat 500 that seemed so small to me, and I asked him jokingly if it was one of his kid's toys. From that time on he called it "the toy" whenever he was talking about it. After frequenting that environment, my desire to leave was growing stronger. I was cleared to register for courses in Florence.

For the most part, I didn't get any encouragement at home. The family showed a certain indifference toward my endeavor, judging it useless. My mother, who wanted above all to keep me near her, was trying to prevent it from happening.

"Other people's countries cast their curse on you. Remember that the foreigner is like the drum of an orchestra, he takes the brunt of the din."

My mother was probably imagining foreign countries as a rough surface and me as a match that, at the first spark, could catch fire. She translated her opposition to my project into benevolent advice. But by then it was useless for her to try to stifle the idea, because now I was determined to follow through.

Perhaps I exaggerated when I answered unappreciatively, thinking that she was uneducated and that her advice was wasted saliva. "Mom, keep in mind that times have changed. We're in a small world now. Small like a village in great-grandfather's day."

Our discussions on this topic seemed to take place in two different centuries since my mother didn't have in mind the present one in which airplanes have shrunk the earthly sphere and made hostile borders irrelevant. And not just air travel: radio, telephone, television, and computers are all potent means that should solidify the hopes of those who aspire to reduce mental distances and achieve peace among people. And these arguments were alien to her.

"The isolation of the past," I used to tell her, "caused the characteristics of every zone on this earth to evolve differently, languages multiplied and each region created its own religion. Isolation leads to rifts, to hostilities...."

From many points of view, and particularly since I had studied a bit, I was convinced that my vision of the world and of life was more level-headed than hers. With her interventions aimed at dissuading me, at making me reconsider, she did nothing but convince me of her ignorance. They had little influence on the course of things and amounted to simple sayings that, at best, had proven true in the past. I challenged them with little effort.

But she is a parent, someone sacred and extraordinary in a person's life, and cannot be let down, so out of maternal respect, I didn't stop treating her well — and only well. Especially since the things she was saying were not lacking in richness. Sometimes I was so amazed by them that I could not ignore their value.

Understanding her concerns, I would have liked to support her, but of course, without canceling my plans. The only path I had left was to defuse her concerns: I dealt with the issue with irony.

The battle my mother conducted was destined to fail. When the moment came, as a believer, and resigned to that outcome, she prayed to God to protect me.

"Then there's no need for you to worry, God's taking care of it. *In the name of Allah, and I believed in Allah, and I trust in Allah...*"

On the eve of my departure, she taught me the five verses that I should recite the moment I walked out the front door. According to her, by reciting them — because in doing so, you turn to God and He listens to you — these verses would protect me until I came back home. I was young, healthy, and a bit of a risk taker. I only believed in what I saw, what I touched, and I had some contempt for non-concrete things.

"And if I don't do it?"

"Don't say that, don't say that!" My mother was getting angry, and in order not to drive her to that point, I stopped short. I listened to her, all ears.

"When you've finished reciting these words of God, the first step you take must be with the right foot."

I ended up learning the verses by heart and I promised to recite them the next morning before leaving the house, even if I wasn't at all convinced I could follow her advice to the letter.

But that night in bed, sleep abandoned me all of a sudden and all the trip's colorful images swirled around in my excited mind. At times it seemed to me that the world I'd reach the following day was all rose-colored, but my mother's pessimism led to gloomy thoughts about the difficulties I'd encounter. By recalling my recently acquired knowledge about the social organization and the cultural level that prevailed there, her worries that were now becoming mine were reduced to problems of daily life. Meanwhile, at regular intervals, my ears buzzed with: *In the name of Allah, and I believed in Allah, and I trust in Allah, no possibilities, no strength without Allah's will, the Highest, and the Greatest.* The night dragged on, sleepless, ignoring my need to be in good shape to face my trip. Fatigue prevailed only as the night was dwindling, and I slept barely three hours.

It wasn't so easy to think of praying in the midst of the confusion caused by all the family members who rushed to greet me in the morning. At the last moment, my mother took me aside. She wanted to tell me one more thing.

"Make sure you don't forget us! Send us a letter at least once a month. Don't forget your family, your country, and above all your religion." She could have gone on giving me endless recommendations that she had already repeated an unreasonable number of times from the moment she became aware of my intentions. I got a bit distracted. Then, getting a hold of myself, I tried to avoid at all cost any chaos on my way out, not only to be in harmony with my promise but also because I truly felt the need for calm now. After saying good-bye to everybody, I had the presence of mind to choose just the right moment: "*In the name of Allah, and I believed in Allah, and I trust in Allah,*" I recited in a faint voice, and I thrust my right foot out the door. The operation was performed by the book, and I felt a sense of relief and satisfaction.

Now it was time to leave behind a piece of myself — my family, my friends, my neighbors and my entire country — for an extended period. Something new and indefinable insinuated itself into my mind, but halfway through the journey, it had already disappeared.

Once I reached my destination, even my mother's advice remained only a fond memory. And I quickly wiped from my mind the image she painted of foreign countries. In my first years, I didn't get involved with figuring out differences related to mentalities. There were so many things to see that kept me from delving into this investigation. I viewed my existence from the practical side so I could live my life more easily, and that's all. From this vantage point, between my own country and my "host" country, I didn't notice a big difference, except perhaps at the material level: the economic development, the order in the city, the wealth of the people, and the high prices that I couldn't afford. I noticed, instead, from the beginning that Italians talked a lot, and often loudly. In general, on the bus or in a bar my fellow countrymen and I spoke as we did back home, so that the conversation wouldn't extend beyond the hearing of our circle. Getting used to the local customs that confronted us every day was a little painful.

"We might as well start talking loudly too," I said once.

"To tell the truth, I can't do it, I mean, I don't dare."

"But when there's nothing to hide…"

I wondered if it was really an Italian characteristic, or if perhaps the issue was with me and my people, laconic and stingy with words. I started thinking about that. I asked myself other somewhat more profound questions; perhaps I shouldn't only go after concrete things. I thought noncommittally about these complex considerations. After all, I was here for my studies, and at their conclusion, I would certainly make my way back home.

Instead, I didn't go back. After two years of temporary accommodations spent in boarding houses, shared rooms and even a few months in a tent at a campground, I had the good fortune to find a home where I stayed for a long time. This allowed me to finish my studies with more ease and more importantly, to live in a neighborhood. With time I even managed to exchange small gifts or be invited to dinner at someone's place.

Mrs. Fossi treated me like a son right from the start. It began at Easter when she gave me a bottle of *spumante* and a homemade pizza. She told me about parts of her life and about her sartorial skills, which she was very proud of.

"Even the marquis had his clothes made by me!"

I remember with great affection poor Mr. Cappelli, so talkative, so Italian. When I met him on the stairs, a conversation of at least twenty minutes always followed. We exchanged opinions, information and, yes, even light-hearted jokes. It was pleasant meeting him on the stairs, even if it wasn't convenient sometimes, especially if I had something to do or if I was about to catch a bus. Mrs. Fossi lived on the floor above me. She had been living alone for years, and every Sunday she went to visit her husband's grave. Mr. Cappelli lived on the floor below me along with his wife. Their children lived in another part of the city. Both of them often asked me if I liked it here in Florence. My limited initial findings on the material side later expanded to include social and cultural behaviors and the relationships that bind one person to another and the individual to society.

At first glance, even in this regard I didn't notice a big difference from the image that I had of my own people. But of course, when digging deeper into the subject, some subtleties could be gleaned from here and there.

My encounters with Mr. Cappelli on the stairs became more frequent. On the other hand, I rarely saw Mrs. Fossi, who was now aging more quickly. Nevertheless, I often heard her repeating with a still-vigorous voice to someone ringing the doorbell, "Who's there? Who's there?"

When I visited her, she treated me affectionately. She always hurried to make coffee, even when I refused it so as not to be a bother.

"You want it with a splash? A little bit of liquor? You want liquor in it?" She was thinking of my pleasure. "Alcohol, do you drink alcohol?" She asked me.

She, a practicing Catholic, would suddenly move from alcohol to questions about my religion. She asked me for the nth time if I was Mohammedan.

"Yes, I am Muslim."

She was rather curious to learn something about it. But discussing religion was never my forte. And I built my life on quite different foundations. Nevertheless I told her what I knew.

"You know, your religion is not like I thought it was. In a way, it is almost the same as ours."

I would answer with a nod, reticent. The truth is that I would have liked to say that people are all alike in their feelings, their pain, and their happiness. But the purpose of my visits wasn't to discuss God and the world, but rather to check on her health. My inability to supply exhaustive answers forced me to stay on a superficial level, and so she moved from one subject to another as usual.

It was thanks to the stairs or to the landings that I got to know the majority of my neighbors: their names, how the families were made up, their origins (often from Tuscany), where their relatives lived. I watched the children grow up from infancy to adolescence.

My relationships expanded beyond the building, they extended into the neighborhood, into bars, stores, and into the numerous repair shops. Seen repeatedly, the faces acquired familiar features, and I don't remember anymore when and how I met one or another. We always greeted each other, swapping jokes. Many of the events that concerned others, concerned me as well.

Mrs. Fossi was often the main reason for meeting. She had reached unmanageable old age. From time to time she would get into some trouble that required help. The first time, distracted by the task of moving a small cabinet in the hallway, because she didn't like where it was, she ended up colliding with the door and falling. She injured her leg. She lost a lot of blood and stained a large part of the floor. Consequently, a bunch of us found ourselves packed in to lend her a hand: one called the ambulance, another cleaned the floor, while she, after the initial shock, remained in bed with her leg stretched out, firing off funny jokes same as always. She showed admirable courage, and after the doctors had checked her over, and the ambulance had left, she wasn't concerned with her leg anymore but felt the need to learn about the people who were there. Seated at her bedside, Mr. Cappelli, who was much younger than she was, treated her like a baby.

"She never listens," he said, patting her lightly on the head. "What should I do with you? I've always told you not to bother with things too heavy for you. The cabinet is not your problem. This one here, she's incorrigible. She doesn't want to listen to my advice."

She wasn't paying any attention to him, jumping from one question to another, and from one topic to another, remembering old conversations, telling stories about her youth, about her work as a seamstress. First she regretted having caused inconvenience, hurrying to offer elegantly-worded apologies, then without realizing it, she expressed in lively tones her pleasure with the company. In the confusion and with all the people intent on taking care of her, Mrs. Fossi was feeling very much at ease. She offered to make coffee for everybody. But the coffee was never made, because we got lost in conversation.

That episode gave rise to a cycle of misadventures for the elderly woman. Her leg didn't heal. It was always wrapped in a bandage. A nurse had to stop by to check on her every day. On several occasions she ended up in the hospital. At home, she continued to have small accidents from time to time. After that lingering injury, there was a kitchen fire and then the broken washing machine that flooded the house.

If Mrs. Fossi's accidents brought the other tenants of the building together, and most of the time involved a bit of fun, no one imagined that one day it would be Mr. Cappelli who would meet the saddest fate. The announcement of his death brought sorrow to everyone's soul.

His bicycle ride around the neighborhood proved fatal. He was hit by a big car and killed on impact. When I heard the terrible news on the stairs where I had shared so many conversations with him, I was paralyzed. I had to struggle to understand what had happened.

The funeral Mass was going to take place in the neighborhood church. I didn't want to miss it. In a somber mood, I hesitantly walked in. The church was full. In addition to the neighbors from the building and those who worked in the neighborhood, there were a lot of people gathered there who I didn't recognize either by sight or by name.

It was the first time I witnessed such a celebration in a sacred place, different from that of my native religion. That didn't disturb me at all. I sat down in the last row of the side aisle. The priest had already begun to speak. I understood all the words of the sermon but I wasn't able to fully understand its meaning.

A strange sensation gave me no respite. I caught a glimpse of Mrs. Cappelli with her relatives, sitting in the first row. Only the deceased's coffin, covered with flowers and golden ribbons, separated them from the priest who, after a long speech, invited the community to stand up several times. I did the same. I took part in the prayer without realizing that I wasn't one of them. I forgot for a moment my origins.

Standing before the remains of Mr. Cappelli, I think that was the best tribute that I could have given him. Getting close to others eliminates a lot of prejudices. Had she been in my place, wouldn't my mother have done the same? At the end of the service, we offered condolences to the family members of the deceased. I followed the others who were calmly speaking to Cappelli's widow. I did the same: words of comfort came to me spontaneously. At that moment I felt deeply what I wanted to say to Mrs. Fossi: that *men's feelings are the same,* not their religions.

I started to confuse the resemblances among people. On the one hand, my mother, my father, and my neighbors at home, and on the other, Mr. Cappelli, Mrs. Fossi, and other acquaintances. They weren't two distinct sides. For me, they were taking the place of one another.

My mind's revolution, planned in Algeria, didn't require huge efforts. I only had to understand the gestures in their genuine meaning, without extraneous interpretations. I obviously wasn't the kind of person who converts to another religion. I believed in something, in small things, things that don't have boundaries either of space or of faith. Small things, valid both here and there, that included me, without making me lose a piece of myself, among these modest and humble people, who grieve, who are moved, who feel joy, just like mine.

Gëzim Hajdari

Contadino della poesia[1]

Fare il contadino della poesia vuol dire tornare all'Essere,
fare il contadino della poesia vuol dire riscoprire le radici,
fare il contadino della poesia vuol dire bere alla fonte,
fare il contadino della poesia vuol dire parlare con i sassi,
fare il contadino della poesia vuol dire ascoltare la terra
fare il contadino della poesia vuol dire rileggere il cielo e la terra,
fare il contadino della poesia vuol dire recuperare i sapori, gli odori,
i colori e i raggi solari mediterranei,
fare il contadino della poesia vuol dire portare nelle narici
i profumi campestri gli odori delle erbe, i canti dei merli,
fare il contadino della poesia vuol dire sapere chinarsi
a raccogliere,
fare il contadino della poesia vuol dire chiamare le cose
per nome come fanno i muratori,
fare il contadino della poesia vuol dire essere un poeta
della campagna,
fare il contadino della poesia vuol dire essere allo stesso tempo
poeta di campagna e di città,
fare il contadino della poesia vuol dire avere un cuore caldo
come la pietra focaia,
fare il contadino della poesia vuol dire mangiare la terra,
fare il contadino della poesia vuol dire lavarsi con la terra,

---

1. Gëzim Hajdari, *Delta del tuo fiume* (Rome: Ensemble, 2015). The version included in this anthology was provided by the author.

Farmer of Poetry

Being a farmer of poetry means going back to Being,
being a farmer of poetry means rediscovering roots,
being a farmer of poetry means drinking at the spring,
being a farmer of poetry means talking with the rocks,
being a farmer of poetry means listening to the earth
being a farmer of poetry means rereading the sky and the earth,
being a farmer of poetry means recovering Mediterranean flavors,
smells, colors and sunshine,
being a farmer of poetry means carrying in your nostrils
the fragrance of fields, the aroma of herbs, the song of blackbirds,
being a farmer of poetry means knowing how to bend down
to harvest,
being a farmer of poetry means calling things
by their names as bricklayers do,
being a farmer of poetry means being a poet
of the countryside,
being a farmer of poetry means being at once
a country poet and a city poet,
being a farmer of poetry means having a heart that is as warm
as flint,
being a farmer of poetry means eating dirt,
being a farmer of poetry means washing with dirt,

fare il contadino della poesia vuol dire essere maledetto dai xhin[2],
fare il contadino della poesia vuol dire disincantarsi dall'industria
culturale che produce libri come scarpe di moda,
fare il contadino della poesia vuol dire creare una poesia come il vino
della vigna, come i fichi d'india, come il pane della campagna,
fare il contadino della poesia vuol dire ridare la dignità perduta
al Verbo,
fare il contadino della poesia vuol dire essere un artigiano della parola,
fare il contadino della poesia vuol dire rispecchiarsi negli occhi della
mucca,
fare il contadino della poesia vuol dire riconoscere nell'asino,
nel cavallo e nella mucca, i nostri antenati,
fare il contadino della poesia vuol dire far sì che i versi abbiano
il profumo inconfondibile del pane caldo a tavola,
fare il contadino della poesia vuol dire guadagnare il piatto
quotidiano col sudore della propria fronte,
fare il contadino della poesia vuol dire sopravvivere alla giornata
lontano dalla patria tradita dai suoi figli indegni,
fare il contadino della poesia vuol dire non possedere nulla
oltre il proprio corpo, non lasciare nulla,
fare il contadino della poesia vuol dire credere nel potere
della poesia come i credenti credono nel potere di dio,
fare il contadino della poesia vuol dire comunicare con dio,
fare il contadino della poesia vuol dire scrivere la propria Bibbia
e il proprio Corano,
fare il contadino della poesia vuol dire tornare all'origine
del messaggio del Verbo,

2. Xhin (djin): anime malvagie che escono di notte e hanno una potenza soprannaturale sugli uomini e sulle cose. Il mito appartiene alle fiabe albanesi di Darsìa.

being a farmer of poetry means being cursed by *xhin*,[1]
being a farmer of poetry means becoming disenchanted with the cultural industry that produces books like fashionable shoes,
being a farmer of poetry means creating poetry that is like vineyard wine, like prickly pears, like country bread,
being a farmer of poetry means restoring lost dignity to
the Word,
being a farmer of poetry means being a craftsman of words,
being a farmer of poetry means seeing yourself in the eyes of the cow,
being a farmer of poetry means recognizing the donkey,
the horse and the cow as your ancestors,
being a farmer of poetry means seeing to it that verses have
the unmistakable fragrance of warm bread on the table,
being a farmer of poetry means earning your daily
meal with the sweat of your brow,
being a farmer of poetry means living hand to mouth
far from the homeland betrayed by her unworthy children,
being a farmer of poetry means not owning anything
but your own body, not leaving anything behind,
being a farmer of poetry means believing in the power
of poetry as believers believe in the power of god,
being a farmer of poetry means communicating with god,
being a farmer of poetry means writing your own *Bible*
and your own *Qur'an*,
being a farmer of poetry means going back to the origins
of the Word's message,

1. Xhin (djin): evil spirits that come out at night and hold supernatural power over people and things. This myth belongs to the Albanian folktales of the Darsìa region. [Author's note: hereafter AN]

fare il contadino della poesia vuol dire ridare la dignità perduta
all'uomo,
fare il contadino della poesia vuol dire ricostruire il tempio
della parola, distrutto dagli eunuchi del minimalismo sterile,
fare il contadino della poesia vuol dire sputare sulle banalità
letterarie contemporanee di Roma, osannate e glorificate dalla mafia
politica e culturale,
fare il contadino della poesia vuol dire scomunicare Roma come
capitale d'Italia,
fare il contadino della poesia vuol dire pisciare sulle poetiche,
fare il contadino della poesia vuol dire produrre poesia, non poetica,
fare il contadino della poesia vuol dire essere poeta, non scrittore di
poesia,
fare il contadino della poesia vuol dire recuperare il senso epico,
musicale e civile della parola,
fare il contadino della poesia vuol dire scrivere in modo semplice
e profondo,
fare il contadino della poesia vuol dire farsi capire come gli epici,
fare il contadino della poesia vuol dire crescere le parole con pazienza
come il giardino cresce le pietre focaie,
fare il contadino della poesia vuol dire scrivere sul proprio corpo
fare il contadino della poesia vuol dire scrivere con il proprio corpo,
fare il contadino della poesia vuol dire vivere il corpo,
fare il contadino della poesia vuol dire essere un poeta
di petto e di pancia, non di testa e di gola,
fare il contadino della poesia vuol dire recuperare la divinità
della parola,
fare il contadino della poesia vuol dire essere libero,
fare il contadino della poesia vuol dire essere un individuo,
fare il contadino della poesia vuol dire non chiedere parole in prestito,

being a farmer of poetry means restoring lost dignity
to man,
being a farmer of poetry means rebuilding the temple
of words, destroyed by the eunuchs of sterile minimalism,
being a farmer of poetry means spitting on the banalities
of contemporary literary Rome, praised and glorified by political
and cultural mafias,
being a farmer of poetry means excommunicating Rome as
Italy's capital,
being a farmer of poetry means pissing on poetics,
being a farmer of poetry means producing poetry not poetics,
being a farmer of poetry means being a poet, not a writer of
poetry,
being a farmer of poetry means recovering the epic,
musical, and civic sense of words,
being a farmer of poetry means writing in a way both simple
and profound,
being a farmer of poetry means being as clear as the epic poets,
being a farmer of poetry means growing words patiently
as the garden grows flint,
being a farmer of poetry means writing on your own body,
being a farmer of poetry means writing with your own body,
being a farmer of poetry means living the body,
being a farmer of poetry means being a poet
with your heart and your gut, not your head and your throat,
being a farmer of poetry means recovering the divinity
of words,
being a farmer of poetry means being free,
being a farmer of poetry means being an individual,
being a farmer of poetry means not borrowing words,

fare il contadino della poesia vuol dire coniare la moneta
del proprio Verbo,
fare il contadino della poesia vuol dire fare della tua nazione
l'Europa,
fare il contadino della poesia vuol dire riconoscersi nella propria
voce,
fare il contadino della poesia vuol dire portare la Voce,
fare il contadino della poesia vuol dire bellezza,
fare il contadino della poesia vuol dire eros,
fare il contadino della poesia vuol dire spingere la gente all'amore,
fare il contadino della poesia vuol dire sedurre come seducono gli
amanti,
fare il contadino della poesia vuol dire essere un amante,
fare il contadino della poesia vuol dire fare l'amore dodici volte
al giorno come una pernice,
fare il contadino della poesia vuol dire essere Uomo,
fare il contadino della poesia vuol dire appartenere alla
razza umana, ed essere se stesso,
fare il contadino della poesia vuol dire essere umano,
fare il contadino della poesia vuol dire tornare al mito,
fare il contadino della poesia vuol dire mettere in moto
il mondo dei sensi,
fare il contadino della poesia vuol dire scendere nel proprio
io centrale tramite gli spiriti e le divinità degli antenati
fare il contadino della poesia vuol dire contropotere,
fare il contadino della poesia vuol dire sfidare l'ordine
dei poteri oscuri,
fare il contadino della poesia vuol dire essere uno scultore
della poesia,

being a farmer of poetry means minting the coin
of your own Word,
being a farmer of poetry means turning your nation
into Europe,
being a farmer of poetry means recognizing yourself in your own
voice,
being a farmer of poetry means bringing Voice,
being a farmer of poetry means beauty,
being a farmer of poetry means eros,
being a farmer of poetry means inspiring people to love,
being a farmer of poetry means seducing the way
lovers do,
being a farmer of poetry means being a lover,
being a farmer of poetry means making love twelve times
a day like a partridge,
being a farmer of poetry means being a Man,
being a farmer of poetry means belonging to the
human race, and being yourself,
being a farmer of poetry means being human,
being a farmer of poetry means returning to myth,
being a farmer of poetry means starting up
the world of the senses,
being a farmer of poetry means descending into your own
inner self through ancestral spirits and divinities,
being a farmer of poetry means counter-power,
being a farmer of poetry means challenging the order
of the dark powers,
being a farmer of poetry means being a sculptor
of poetry,

fare il contadino della poesia vuol dire rischiare per la propria poesia,
fare il contadino della poesia vuol dire resistere,
fare il contadino della poesia vuol dire nutrire la propria parola
con il proprio sangue,
fare il contadino della poesia vuol dire diventare carne e sangue
delle proprie parole,
fare il contadino della poesia vuol dire essere un rivoluzionario,
fare il contadino della poesia vuol dire leggere la Storia
con i propri occhi e conoscere la ControStoria,
fare il contadino della poesia vuol dire misurarsi con la Storia,
non con i propri coglioni,
fare il contadino della poesia vuol dire essere un 'eretico',
fare il contadino della poesia vuol dire non scendere mai a patti
con i boia dell'umanità,
fare il contadino della poesia vuol dire demistificare i pseudo miti
del realismo socialista che hanno servito il regime comunista
e la lotta di classe in Albania,
fare il contadino della poesia vuol dire raccontare sempre la verità,
fare il contadino della poesia vuol dire interpretare il mondo
dalla mia Darsìa[3]*,*
fare il contadino della poesia vuol dire parlare all'Europa
da balcanico,
fare il contadino della poesia vuol dire cogliere l'Assoluto,
la solitudine di dio e il mistero dell'esistenza,
fare il contadino della poesia vuol dire creare un dio a propria somiglianza,
fare il contadino della poesia vuol dire saper leggere nel fango,

---

3. Darsìa: provincia collinosa dove è nato l'autore, situata nel Nord-est della città di Lushnje, in Albania.

being a farmer of poetry means taking chances on your own
poetry,
being a farmer of poetry means resisting,
being a farmer of poetry means nourishing your own words
with your own blood,
being a farmer of poetry means becoming flesh and blood
of your own words,
being a farmer of poetry means being a revolutionary,
being a farmer of poetry means reading History
with your own eyes and knowing CounterHistory,
being a farmer of poetry means measuring yourself by History
not by your own balls,
being a farmer of poetry means being a "heretic,"
being a farmer of poetry means never coming to terms
with humanity's executioners,
being a farmer of poetry means demystifying the pseudo myths
of socialist realism that served the communist regime
and class warfare in Albania,
being a farmer of poetry means always telling the truth,
being a farmer of poetry means interpreting the world
from my Darsìa,[2]
being a farmer of poetry means speaking to Europe
as a Balkan,
being a farmer of poetry means grasping the Absolute,
god's solitude and the meaning of existence,
being a farmer of poetry means creating a god in your own
image,
being a farmer of poetry means knowing how to read, in the mud,

2. Darsìa: the hilly province where the author was born, located northeast of the city of Lushnje, in Albania. [AN]

nel freddo, nel gelo, nel silenzio nella solitudine, nella polvere
che ci circonda, il mistero del proprio destino,
fare il contadino della poesia vuol dire raccontare la ferita mortale
dell'uomo svuotato dalla dittatura del denaro,
fare il contadino della poesia vuol dire essere un Geremia,[4]
fare il contadino della poesia vuol dire tornare all'oggettività
della poesia,
fare il contadino della poesia vuol dire creare ogni giorno,
con la punta del coltello, sulla propria pelle, una nuova patria
e morire altrove,
fare il contadino della poesia vuol dire scegliere l'esilio invece
di asservirsi al potere,
fare il contadino della poesia vuol dire essere un esule
esiliato nell'esilio,
fare il contadino della poesia vuol dire essere un guerriero epico,
fare il contadino della poesia vuol dire essere padrone di sé stesso,
fare il contadino della poesia vuol dire amare la vita,
fare il contadino della poesia vuol dire essere un martire del desiderio
della parola,
fare il contadino della poesia vuol dire essere un 'kamikaze' d'amore,
fare il contadino della poesia vuol dire sentirsi parte della totalità,
fare il contadino della poesia vuol dire insegnare a tutti ad essere
esuli e stranieri per condividere insieme destini e futuri,
fare il contadino della poesia vuol dire essere un uomo di besa,[5]

---

4. Geremia (650–586), profeta e grande poeta, testimone della crisi dello Stato di Giuda, visse con dolore la conquista di Gerusalemme da parte di Nabucodonosor, il re della Babilonia; lottò contro re, contro preti, falsi profeti, traditori, avrebbe voluto la pace e la fratellanza e invece ottenne guerre, deportazioni, massacri.

5. La *besa* oppure *Fjala e dhanum* significa sicurezza, ma anche tregua ed alleanza. È la fede giurata, la parola data per gli albanesi.

in the cold, in the frost, in silence and solitude, in the dust
that surrounds us, the mystery of your own existence,
being a farmer of poetry means narrating the fatal wounding
of man, gutted by the tyranny of money,
being a farmer of poetry means being a Jeremiah,[3]
being a farmer of poetry means returning to the objectivity
of poetry,
being a farmer of poetry means creating every single day,
with a knife tip, on your own skin, a new homeland
and dying elsewhere,
being a farmer of poetry means choosing exile instead
of becoming a slave to power,
being a farmer of poetry means being an exile
exiled in exile,
being a farmer of poetry means being an epic warrior,
being a farmer of poetry means being the master of yourself,
being a farmer of poetry means loving life,
being a farmer of poetry means being a martyr to the desire
of words,
being a farmer of poetry means being a "kamikaze" of love,
being a farmer of poetry means feeling a part of the whole,
being a farmer of poetry means teaching all people to be
exiles and strangers so as to share destinies and futures together,
being a farmer of poetry means being a man of *besa*,[4]

---

3. Jeremiah (650-586): a prophet and a great poet, who witnessed the crisis of the State of Judah and suffered the conquest of Jerusalem by Nebuchadnezzar, king of Babylon. He fought against kings, priests, false prophets, and traitors. He wished for peace and brotherhood but instead experienced wars, deportations, and massacres. [AN]

4. *Besa,* or *Fjala e dhanum,* means safety, but also truce and alliance. For Albanians, it is the sworn faith, the promise. [AN]

la parola d'onore per i montanari della mia stirpe antica shqiptar,[6]
fare il contadino della poesia vuol dire giurare non in nome di dio,
ma in nome della besa, come fanno da secoli i miei avi malsor[7]
delle Bjeshkët të Nëmuna[8]
fare il contadino della poesia vuol dire vivere al confine
ubriaco di mondi,
fare il contadino della poesia vuol dire essere un vero bektashi,[9]
fare il contadino della poesia vuol dire essere un profeta,
fare il contadino della poesia vuol dire essere condannati
per il proprio profetare,
fare il contadino della poesia vuol dire camminare sulle orme
di Gilgamesh, Omero, Li Po, Rumi, Virgilio, Milton, Hugo,
Whitman, Mandelstam, Tagore, Achmatova, Lorca e Soynka,
fare il contadino della poesia vuol dire essere chiamato traditore
e nemico della patria, per aver denunciato i crimini e gli abusi
della dittatura di Enver Hoxha[10] *e dei recenti regimi postcomunisti*
mafiosi di Sali Berisha[11] *e di Fatos Nano*[12],

---

6. *Shqiptar:* albanese.

7. *Malsor:* montanari delle Alpi, da dove proviene anche la stirpe del poeta.

8. Bjeshkët të Nëmuna: Montagne Maledette, situate nel nord d'Albania, dove ha regnato per 500 anni il *Kanun,* Codice Giuridico Orale Albanese.

9. Confraternita mistica dell'Albania, seguace di Jalal al Din Rum (1207–73) cui appartiene la tradizione familiare del poeta.

10. Enver Hoxha (1908–85), uno dei dittatori comunisti più spietati d'Europa. Fu segretario del Partito Comunista Albanese. Governò l'Albania dalla fine della Seconda guerra mondiale fino alla sua morte.

11. Sali Ram Berisha (1944). Ex-segretario del Partito Comunista di Enver Hoxha, nonché cardiologo facente parte dello staff dei medici che prendevano cura dei membri del *Politburo* del regime. È stato primo Ministro (2005–13), nonché Presidente della Repubblica d'Albania postcomunista (tra il 1992 e il 1997).

12. Fatos Nano (1952): figlio di Thanas Nano (direttore della Radio Televisione durante il regime comunista di Enver Hoxha), e di Maria Nano, ricercatrice

word of honor for highlanders of my ancient *shqiptar*[5] stock,
being a farmer of poetry means swearing not in the name of god,
but in the name of the besa, according to the centuries-old custom
of my *malsor*[6] ancestors of the Bjeshkët të Nëmuna,[7]
being a farmer of poetry means living on drunken
world boundaries,
being a farmer of poetry means being a true *bektashi*,[8]
being a farmer of poetry means being a prophet,
being a farmer of poetry means being condemned
for your prophesizing,
being a farmer of poetry means walking in the footprints
of Gilgamesh, Homer, Li Po, Rumi, Virgil, Milton, Hugo,
Whitman, Mandelstam, Tagore, Achmatova, Lorca, and Soynka,
being a farmer of poetry means being called a traitor
and an enemy of the homeland for denouncing the crimes and abuses
committed by the dictatorship of Enver Hoxha[9] and the recent
post-communist mafia regimes of Sali Berisha[10] and Fatos Nano,[11]

---

5. *Shqiptar*: Albanian. [AN]

6. *Malsor*: highlanders of the Alps, where the poet's lineage originated. [AN]

7. Bjeshkët të Nëmuna: Cursed Mountains, located in northern Albania, where *Kanun,* the Albanian Oral Code, has been the law of the land for five hundred years. [AN]

8. Albanian mystical order, followers of Jalal al Din Rum (1207–73), to which the poet's family tradition belongs. [AN]

9. Enver Hoxha (1908–85): one of Europe's most brutal dictators. He served as secretary of the Albanian Communist Party. He ruled over Albania from the end of the Second World War until his death. [AN]

10. Sali Ram Berisha (1944–): a former secretary of Enver Hoxha's Communist Party and a cardiologist, member of the medical staff who provided care for the members of the regime's *Politburo*. He served as Prime Minister (2005–13), as well as president of the post-Communist Republic of Albania (from 1992 to 1997). [AN]

11. Fatos Nano (1952–): son of Thanas Nano (director of Radio and Television Broadcasting under the communist regime of Enver Hoxha), and Maria Nano

fare il contadino della poesia vuol dire non accettare premi letterari
e altre onorificenze dai governanti albanesi di oggi/di ieri,
in quanto responsabili della tragedia comunista,
fare il contadino della poesia vuol dire essere antinazionalista,
fare il contadino della poesia vuol dire essere 'antialbanese',
fare il contadino della poesia vuol dire non avere lettori nel tuo Paese d'origine,
fare il contadino della poesia vuol dire scrivere in italiano e tormentarsi in albanese,
fare il contadino della poesia vuol dire essere ignorato cinicamente
nel proprio Paese di origine dalla mafia politica e culturale,
fare il contadino della poesia vuol dire attendere mezzo secolo,
per essere invitato a presentare la propria opera in Albania,
fare il contadino della poesia vuol dire identificarsi con il dolore
del tuo popolo,
fare il contadino della poesia vuol dire memoria,
fare il contadino della poesia vuol dire far ricordare a te stesso
che il compito del Poeta è quello di rendere un'epoca consapevole
dei propri ideali,
fare il contadino della poesia vuol dire essere solo come Dante Alighieri ed Ezra Pound,
fare il contadino della poesia vuol dire recuperare il legame,
tra pagina bianca e onestà intellettuale, tra parola e verità, tra poesia e vita,
fare il contadino della poesia significa versi nati dalla vita
e non allevati in serra, o nelle scuole di scrittura,
fare il contadino della poesia vuol dire diffidare dell'arte
isterica, balbuziente, autoreferenziale dei metropolitani alienati,

---

presso l'Istituto di Studi Marxisti-leninisti. F. Nano è stato diverse volte primo ministro dell'Albania postcomunista.

being a farmer of poetry means not accepting literary prizes
and any other awards from present and past Albanian rulers,
responsible for the communist tragedy,
being a farmer of poetry means being anti-nationalist,
being a farmer of poetry means being "anti-Albanian,"
being a farmer of poetry means not having readers in your Country
of origin,
being a farmer of poetry means writing in Italian and agonizing
in Albanian,
being a farmer of poetry means being cynically ignored
by political and cultural mafias in your Country of origin,
being a farmer of poetry means waiting half a century
to be invited to present your work in Albania,
being a farmer of poetry means identifying with the grief
of your people,
being a farmer of poetry means memory,
being a farmer of poetry means reminding yourself
that the poet's task is to make an epoch aware
of its ideals,
being a farmer of poetry means being alone like Dante Alighieri
and Ezra Pound,
being a farmer of poetry means recovering the bond,
between blank page and intellectual honesty, word and truth,
poetry and life,
being a farmer of poetry means verses sprouted from life,
not bred in a greenhouse or in writing schools,
being a farmer of poetry means distrusting the hysterical,
stammering, self-referential art of alienated urbanites,

(researcher at the Institute for Marxist-Leninist Studies). He served as Prime Minister of post-Communist Albania several times. [AN]

fare il contadino della poesia vuol dire recuperare i veri valori
etici e la tradizione,
fare il contadino della poesia vuol dire gioia e dolore, vita e impegno,
nella vita, non nel linguaggio,
fare il contadino della poesia vuol dire essere cacciato fuori dalla Curia
dei poeti ufficiali di Roma, per aver denunciato, nel 2003, insieme al
poeta Luigi Manzi, la corruzione, gli scambi di favori e le ruberie
della vecchia Gestione del Centro Internazionale Eugenio Montale,
fare il contadino della poesia vuol dire abitare fuori dalle gerarchie
letterarie ufficiali, perché i veri poeti non accettano compromessi
e scambi di favori,
fare il contadino della poesia vuol dire essere un poeta antico,
fare il contadino della poesia vuol dire essere un vero contadino,
fare il contadino della poesia vuol dire essere un intellettuale.
fare il contadino della poesia vuol dire scrivere non per essere
creduto, ma per il popolo e per quelli che verranno,
fare il contadino della poesia vuol dire contribuire al beneficio
dell'umanità,
fare il contadino della poesia vuol dire essere un pastore di parole,
fare il contadino della poesia vuol dire salvezza,
fare il contadino della poesia vuol dire vivere negli altri,
fare il contadino della poesia vuol dire attraversare la vita,
fare il contadino della poesia vuol dire essere uno straniero di passaggio.

being a farmer of poetry means recovering true ethical
values and tradition,
being a farmer of poetry means joy and grief, life and commitment,
in life not in language,
being a farmer of poetry means being expelled from the Curia
of Rome's official poets for denouncing, in 2003, with the
poet Luigi Manzi, the corruption, back-scratching, and graft
of the old Management of the Eugenio Montale International Center,
being a farmer of poetry means living outside official
literary hierarchies because true poets don't accept compromise
and back-scratching,
being a farmer of poetry means being an ancient poet,
being a farmer of poetry means being a true farmer,
being a farmer of poetry means being an intellectual,
being a farmer of poetry means writing not to be
believed, but for the people and those who will come,
being a farmer of poetry means contributing to the benefit
of humanity,
being a farmer of poetry means shepherding words,
being a farmer of poetry means salvation,
being a farmer of poetry means living in others,
being a farmer of poetry means going through life,
being a farmer of poetry means being a passing foreigner.

Pap Khouma

Figlio[1]

È nato mio figlio da te
è nero come l'ebano
è bianco tutto bianco.

È tuo è mio.

Figlio del caso
o frutto maturo dell'amore
mio figlio è già nato da te
ma non è nero
e neppure bianco.

Ha il colore indefinibile
di questo tramonto che fa male
solo agli occhi di un ipocrita.

Mio figlio è qua
ma non è di qui
né di altrove.

Ha attraversato la frontiera
di tutti i colori e non ha
niente di strano.

Questo bambino che
ci assomiglia non è tuo

---

1. "Figlio" was published in *Africa Italia: Due continenti si avvicinano,* edited by Sante Matteo and Stefano Bellucci (Santarcangelo di Romagna (RI): Fara Editore, 1999); "Ombra" appeared in *El Ghibli, rivista online di letteratura della migrazione* 6.27 (March 2010). The versions included in this anthology were provided by the author.

Son

My son was born of you
he is black like ebony
he is white, all white.

He is yours he is mine.

Child of chance
or ripe fruit of love
my son is now born of you
but he isn't black
nor is he white.

He is the indefinable color
of this sunset, which hurts
only a hypocrite's eyes.

My son is here
but he is not from around here
nor is he from somewhere else.

He has crossed the borders
of all colors and nothing
about him is strange.

This child who is our likeness
is neither yours

neppure mio
appartiene solo al domani.

Mio figlio è di tutti i colori
e a nessuno assomiglia.

A domani figlio.

Milano 1991

nor mine
he belongs only to tomorrow.

My son is every color
and he is nobody's likeness.

Until tomorrow son.

Milan 1991

Ombra

È l'altro lo vedi
quello là venuto
da fuori come un pescatore
senza bussola su una piroga
con gli ormeggi rotti

È lui quello là
in balia di un mare
capriccioso di un
tempo agitato
vento di sabbie
tempeste di neve

È il tuo vicino di casa
lo vedi quello là
il cui nome sembra
strano e la sua parlata
di laggiù disturba

È l'altro lo sai
questa palma del Teneré
venuta a piantarsi nel
tuo giardino nel Tevere
cambiando per sempre
il paesaggio

È l'altro quello là
diventato te legato allo
stesso carro dal destino
e mai più te ne separerai

Milano 1991

Shadow

He is the other you see
that guy who has come
from the outside like a fisherman
without a compass in a canoe
with broken moorings

He is that guy
at the mercy
of a capricious sea
of an unsettled season
sandstorms
blizzards

He is your neighbor
you see that guy
with his strange sounding name
and his language from down there
that is so disturbing

He is the other you know it
this palm from the Ténéré
come to put down roots
in your garden on the Tiber
forever changing
the landscape

He is the other
that guy who has become you
hitched to the same wagon by destiny
and never again to be parted from you

Milan 1991

Kossi Komla-Ebri

Two Matchboxes[1]

When the dark night comes
Words will falter
We won't be able to cheat insomnia
With our dreams any more.

When the dark night comes
Entwining our desires
My rough hands
Will shower your womb
With petals of regret

Love,
Before the dark night comes
Give me a pastel child
A watercolor child…
To brighten the dark night.

On the way back from the cemetery Francesca's mother had suggested unconvincingly: "Stay with us for a while…"

Knowing her daughter, she already knew the answer.

"No! No, Mom. I'm fine, don't worry, besides…life goes on."

Then, caressing her protruding belly, she repeated with even greater sweetness: "Life goes on."

And so on the day after her husband's funeral, Francesca Marelli woke up from a dreamless sleep. Without a glance at the

1. Kossi Komla-Ebri, "Due scatole di fiammiferi," in *Anime in viaggio: La nuova mappa dei popoli* (Rome: Adnkronos, 2001).

empty place beside her, she got up quickly despite her advanced state of pregnancy.

In the bathroom, at the sight of the two toothbrushes, the thought of her husband violently pierced her heart. Compelling and clear, the vivid memory of his tender voice on the day of their wedding: "Francy, I, Togbé, only son of Atsu Kwami and Ami Dzatugbé, swear that my heart will be yours forever."

Francesca passed an icy hand over her face to chase away that voice. She dressed in a hurry. She took one of the two matchboxes that were in the dresser drawer. On the desk, she found a padded envelope, the kind with bubble cushioning. Francesca clutched the matchbox and, before putting it inside the envelope, pressed it to her heart and kissed it. After sealing the parcel, she addressed it to her in-laws and left for the post office to mail it to Atsu and Ami.

From the stories her husband told her, Francesca knew that:

> *...four times already Atsu and Ami had seen their dream of having children dashed, at the third, seventh, eighth, and ninth months. Some men argued that Atsu's blood was too strong. Atsu's aunts proposed finding him a second wife. Certain women at the market whispered furtively pointing at Kuno, the old woman who lived alone at the edge of the village. There were rumors that the elderly woman could devour babies in their mothers' womb with her very eyes in order to indulge her fetishes.*
>
> *After trying all sorts of potions and various ritual sacrifices, Atsu and Ami then decided to consult the soothsayer to learn why their children were dying. That way they could eliminate the evil that was destroying them and figure out if it was a spell cast by a witchdoctor. At the end of the divination ceremony, the man gave Ami some herbs to chew during pregnancy, and decoctions for morning baths to be taken in water that had rested under a full moon. He also prescribed performing the ceremony of the 'hidden baby' at birth.*

So one Friday morning, Atsu's wife, who hadn't had a period in nine months, went up to the ancestors and, without disturbing the ants and mice in the thatched roofs of the village with her pains, came back with a strong baby boy.

When Ami's labor started, and she was about to give birth, the old village midwife told young Djifa to go hide in the bush not far from the houses where the paths that led to the field and the river intersected.

The newborn baby was separated from the placenta: the real 'mother' that the boy's aunts went to bury according to instructions, so as to give the couple the chance of having more children in the future. The midwife placed the swaddled baby in a basket, which she then laid down by the river near Djifa's hiding place. As soon as she heard a passerby approaching, the woman took two steps as if to leave. Suddenly the passerby was heard uttering cries of surprise: "I've found a baby! I've found a baby!"

At that moment Djifa sneaked out of his hiding place, also shouting for joy and jumping around in a way that defies description. All the people from the nearby huts came running, and together they all returned home. The person who found the newborn became a pretend kin to the baby, and consequently gave him a name. He returned the baby to the midwife saying: "Coming back from the fields, I found this little one. I've come to entrust him to you. Take good care of him so that he may grow in health and wisdom. Since I found him, we will name him 'Fofoè,' that is to say 'foundling.'"

They also gave him the name Koffi because he was born on a Friday.

After this ceremony, he was safe.

"So why do you go by Togbé?" Francesca asked him impatiently.

"Hold on, Francy, let me tell the story…"

(Togbé loved telling stories, savoring the words in his mouth, narrating in great detail, to the point of mimicking, at times, the various protagonists of his stories, playing them in different tones of voice.)

"A boy! A beautiful baby boy!" the midwife's joyous cheer went up from the hut amid the infant's cries.

"My God, he looks so much like my late brother!" said Aunt Afi.

"Yes, he's the spitting image of Kuaku!" confirmed old Osofo with his toothless grin.

Emotion and pride spread over the usually imperturbable face of young Atsu.

Surely, everything would have been perfect were it not for the fact that the baby refused to nurse and kept on crying. After three days his skin had become so wrinkled up that you could count his ribs with the naked eye. He cried every night without getting any sleep and kept everyone else from getting any, either.

His parents and aunts, after a week of this living hell, began thinking about searching for the cause of their little heir's endless laments.

"Let's go to the soothsayer! Let's hurry," said Aunt Afi, "because a tree can hide a forest."

"Surely he'll be able to identify our son's 'dzoto' [guardian ancestor]," declared Uncle Atsutsè in a serious voice.

During the divination séance, the spirit of Grandpa Kuaku took possession of the body of the trance-like soothsayer to proclaim: "Koffi is my son's son and yet he is his father's father because he is my reincarnation. Go to my hut. You'll find my armlet hanging on a wall. Put it around his neck and cover him with my ceremonial kente cloth for six months, and then I'll be able to come back to live among you."

Koffi stopped crying that same night, and he began suckling his mother's breasts, and soon after he regained weight.

For the occasion, Atsu organized a dinner inviting his entire large family to take part, to eat and drink to welcome the little boy that they all, from that day, began to call 'Togbé,' that is, 'grandpa.'

"That's why you're called Togbé!" beamed Francesca.

Ignoring her interruption, her husband continued imperturbably:

At dawn on the eighth day after my birth, Uncle Atsutsé took me to Elder Agbanavon for the rite of circumcision. An uncircumcised boy, according to tradition, will never become a man. There was no need for Uncle to warn him, as tradition recommended, not to lie with a woman the night before because it would bring misfortune upon the ceremony. The wise Agbanavon used to claim that not even the hottest memories could warm his blood anymore.

Once we arrived at the elder's abode, I was carried in front of the hut with the tron, the ancestors' voodoo, by the entry. I was sprinkled with succulents wet with dew collected in the clay basin sitting on top of three crossed logs at the entrance to the ceremonial room…

That day, concluded Togbé, I became a man ready to face his Sé [destiny].

≈

Nobody knew, back then, that destiny would bring him to cross the ocean, that water that boils without needing any fire, in an iron bird. Nobody could have imagined that there, in the land of people with white skin, he would meet the love of his life and… his death.

Nor was Francesca Marelli expecting to meet the man she would fall in love with at first sight and that cruel fate would snatch him away after barely two years together. Inevitably, the memory of the train ride from Milan to Asso resurfaced. She could see again his noble face absorbed in reading a French magazine. The only empty seat was there, next to him. When she approached him, he raised his head for a moment and they locked eyes. She caught herself asking in French:

"C'est libre?"

It felt like magic seeing such a seemingly serious face light up with a childlike smile, so disarming that it pulled on your heartstrings.

"*Oui!* How is it that you speak French?"

She explained that she was finishing a degree in languages at the University of Milan. He expressed his surprise, remarking how rare it was to meet Italians who spoke Molière's language so well. Three years before, when he had arrived in Italy, given its proximity to France, he was convinced of quite the opposite. She blushed with pleasure at his compliment.

Just before reaching Meda,[2] when she told him that her name was Francesca, he remarked: "Francesca, Françoise…it's clear that France, the French language, really is in your destiny."

They talked as if they had known each other for a long time. Withdrawn and reserved by all accounts, she caught herself confiding her dreams. And in the time it took to get to Canzo,[3] Francesca learned that he was from Togo and had left his homeland to teach French in neighboring Ghana. He had subsequently left for Senegal and the Ivory Coast where he taught English, and afterwards for Libya where he met some Italians and then travelled with them to Italy. Now he was working in a Canzo factory where they made scissors.

2. A train stop about halfway on the rail line Milan–Asso.

3. The train stop before Asso.

When Togbé got off at Canzo, even though she was headed to Asso, she got off with him, and they walked together to the next stop.

Francesca remembers that when she got home that evening, her mother inspected her closely during dinner with that instinct only a mother possesses, before asking: "What's up with you today? You look funny!"

"Me? Nothing, Mom, same old stuff."

So many train rides! Encounters made up of words, of silence and of listening, all followed by prying eyes and playful grins brimming with innuendo, but also many smiles of affectionate understanding.

♒

That night — a night of dense fog — after a fevered Togbé closed his eyes on this life, Francesca sat down, curling up by the fireplace. Desperate, she was searching for some warmth to heat up her soul, chilled with grief. She watched the blue flames spring up and observed them as they burst into orange–yellow flames, feverishly licking the dry wood that merrily crackled with a thousand sparks, making the logs glow bright red. They slowly blackened, smoldering. When the flame appeared about to die out, all it took was a twig to poke it and bring it back to life.

Mustering her courage, she picked up the phone and called Togbé's parents in Africa. In the silence of the night, all the way from Africa, clear, quiet, and sweet, the incredibly young voice of Togbé's mother reached Francesca's ears. Upon hearing the terrible news, she uttered only a soft gasp: "Oh!"

After a long silence, the elderly Ami asked in a hoarse voice: "My child, where are you now?"

"I'm here, alone, at our home, by the fireplace. I felt like being alone."

"I understand..."

After a long pause filled with sighs and suppressed tears, she continued: "You see, my child, our lives are like those of the logs in the fire pit, all it takes is a puff of air to kindle them...some burn generating light and warmth for a long time, others produce a lot of smoke and nothing else...but all it takes is a puff of air to put them out or rekindle them...and so it is for our lives...it all depends on our *Sé*."

The elderly Ami took a deep breath and continued: "My daughter, it's sad for a mother to survive her own son. You know, a child is a dream filled with many dreams, cause of much grief, sleepless nights, and agonies over the slightest fever. But a child is joy, a privilege for us women, a gift from *Sé*. *Sé* gives and *Sé* takes back. That's the way it is. Many suffer because of distance, but for a mother a child is never far away because he is always with her in her heart. Loved ones die only when we forget them. Togbé's *Sé* wanted him back, and it was like tearing him out of my heart, but I know that a baby is growing in your womb, that my son hasn't died, instead his seed has gone beyond time, beyond the ocean, and will bear fruit under other skies, which in turn will bear many other fruits in many parts of the earth. I take pride in this today. I am proud because part of me will see things I don't know about, and that I don't even dare to dream of. Don't be afraid: his — our — blood is strong..."

She concluded by saying: "Did my son tell you what to do?"

"Yes, he told me about the matchbox."

"Good. I'm sending you a big hug. Be strong! We'll be waiting. Here is his father, he wants to talk to you."

When the call was over, Francesca, mindful of the directions she had received, took a pair of scissors and approached the lifeless body of her companion.

Carefully, she cut his nails and hair, divided them in two parts, wrapped them in two small squares of white cloth and placed them in two matchboxes. She prepared a package, ready for shipment to his family back home.

Togbé always used to say: "If I should die here in your country, please don't waste money to send my body back home. Wherever one dies, the flesh dissolves in the ground for good. You will send only my nails and hair because we believe that they are the repositories of vital energy, since they alone continue to grow throughout the whole life course. The incorporeal and immortal soul, after forty days, will rejoin relatives and friends in *Tséfe*.[4] Please, just let my family know, so that they may have a funeral, lest my soul remain lost, silent, wandering and forlorn, and unable to participate in the joys of the afterlife. My living breath, instead, will continue to roam until it's able to be reincarnated one day in the body of a new baby born into my family."

Francesca didn't like this kind of talk and she tried to avoid it, to shut him up by saying: "Come on! Stop it. You know this stuff scares me!"

But he went on, in a calm and deep voice, as if she hadn't interrupted him: "You see, my love, even though we are born to die, even if life belongs to death, death is never an end in itself. We are nothing but souls on a never-ending journey…"

That day Francesca Marelli went out to mail her matchbox.

≈

In due time, Francesca gave birth to a healthy baby boy. At his birth, Francesca's mother, who had accompanied her to the maternity ward, looked at her grandchild raising her eyebrows, and exclaimed: "But…he's white!"

Francesca was left speechless for a moment, then burst out laughing so hard she had tears in her eyes, and finally explained: "Of course, Mom. Don't worry. He's Togbé's child. He'll get his caffe latte complexion in two or three days or so."

4. The land of the dead.

She named him Apélété, as her father-in-law Atsu had suggested during their brief phone conversation: "You see, Francesca, our son departed leaving your home empty, insecure, and in despair. When the fruit that you now carry in your womb is born, if it's a boy you must call him Apélété, which means 'the home is standing,' and if it's a girl you must call her Ahuefa, which means 'peace is in the home.' These are our customs, and you'll see that you'll go back to living."

But in the first days after the baby's birth, anguish made its home in the inner recesses of Francesca's soul. Little Apélété drove the nurses crazy and kept the entire nursery awake with his cries. He wanted nothing to do with breast-feeding and refused the formula they tried to give him with the bottle.

The doctors were seriously concerned with his "weight loss beyond the physiological limit" and considered putting him on an I.V.

On the third night, Francesca had a dream about her departed companion and everything became crystal clear to her, like water flowing cheerfully over stones.

When she woke up, she called home asking her mother to bring one of her husband's shirts. After her mother complied, she went to the nursery where little Apélété was screaming uncontrollably, blue in the face. And there, under the stunned and surprised looks of the staff, she calmly laid the shirt over the child. It was like a miracle: hiccupping, he calmed down and stopped screaming. Francesca picked him up, and he finally latched on to his mother's breast, suckling voraciously.

Soon thereafter, he fell blissfully asleep in his crib, his fists clenched and his arms outstretched above his head under her loving gaze.

Francesca's mother stared at the infant in disbelief:

"My God! He looks so much like his father!"

"Yes," nodded Francesca with an enigmatic and mysterious smile, before adding: "He truly is my Togbé."

When Francesca came home from the hospital, her mother saw her bury a matchbox in the garden, under the tree where her husband, during the summer, used to take his afternoon nap.

"What's that, Francesca?" she asked.

"Nothing! Nothing, Mom, just life going on."

"My child…I think you've become like them."

"You think so?… Yes, perhaps a little."

Gabriella Kuruvilla

The House[1]

I worked on it for days, at night. I used a pencil to draw it on paper, bent over the table, ruler and eraser in hand, the old-fashioned way. Nowadays houses come to life inside computers and suddenly appear on the ground, wherever that ground may be: Swiss chalets in Africa and Chinese pagodas in France.

Today that house, which was supposed to shelter all of us, is a picture on the wall. It's acrylic on canvas, not bricks in Trivandrum.[2]

It has remained a dream, never realized. It was for your return to India, that never happened. You always talked about wanting to go back, but never did. You deceived yourself. We can't be honest with others if we lie to ourselves, that's obvious. But you didn't know that you were pretending.

You died in Italy, in Busto Arsizio, surrounded by cherry and peach trees, in the garden of your golden years, although you imagined ending your days among mango and papaya trees, in your childhood garden.

You'd ask me to design a multi-storied building: a kitchen, a pantry, a living room, a laundry, a bathroom, and seven bedrooms, all with private baths.

---

1. Gabriella Kuruvilla, "La casa," in *È la vita, dolcezza* (Milan: Baldini Castoldi Dalai, 2008; Milan: Morellini, 2014). An earlier version of the story, entitled "Documenti," was one of the winners of the third edition of the Lingua Madre Literary Prize (2007), and has been published in *Lingua Madre Duemilasette,* ed. Daniela Finocchi (Turin: Edizioni SEB27, 2007).

2. Trivandrum (or Thiruvananthapuram) is the capital of the southern Indian state of Kerala.

I'd tell you, "It sounds like a hotel."

You'd answer, "Design it for me."

You wanted me to become an architect. You had seen me study to become one, and I finally got the degree, but I've designed only that one house, which has remained a dream, never realized. Just like your return to India.

I took some black acrylic and painted walls, doors, windows, and furnishings on a huge canvas. Today your Indian house is a 78x78 inch picture, hanging in my living room.

I had to go back to your Italian house, in Busto Arsizio. I needed reality in order to forget the dream. And find you again the way you were, not the way I imagine you. I imagine you naked and barefoot, with a cloth wrapped around your waist to cover just your private parts, sitting cross-legged: pretty much like Gandhi.

They laid you inside a coffin dressed in shirt, trousers, and shoes. And with a Swatch on your wrist. In case you ever want to know what time it is, underground.

I had to go back to your Italian house, in Busto Arsizio.

The kitchen full of appliances, tableware, food and beverages, is exactly the way it was when you, with your white apron hanging on your black skin, used to cook, set the table, clear it, wash and tidy up while listening and dancing to the music of Bob Dylan.

You'd say, "It's ready, sit down."

And the four of us kids dropped what we were doing, entered your kingdom, and ate up your food, which for us was always the best. Your risotto Milanese was excellent, perfect: never undercooked and never overcooked. Simply perfect.

Now the kitchen is exactly the way it used to be when you were here, except that it looks like a photograph. The photograph of a motionless, odorless landscape, with the living subject missing. You, my father.

I walk in, I try to touch furniture and move objects. I try to be you, to make you live again in my gestures. I offer my body as a simulacrum of your life. I am your puppet. But I am not you, and I miss you even more since I have been trying to reproduce you. I stop this morbid pantomime right away. I don't cook, I don't set the table, I don't clear it, I don't wash, I don't tidy up. I don't eat either: I'm not hungry. I haven't been for three days. I haven't been hungry since the funeral.

Like out of a Hollywood movie, the four of us children stood by your casket, two on one side and two on the other, dressed in black and with our heads bowed. Each one of us held an umbrella in our right hand since of course it was raining that day. Raindrops were falling on my neck and running down my back. It was uncomfortable. They covered you with sopping wet dirt and flowers. Then they secured you with a stone, so you can't get out even if you try. You are sealed in the underground world. At the mercy of the worms, I fear.

Now the sun is shining outside, an unwelcome guest. It has shamelessly made its way into your Italian home: the real one, not the one in your dream, fiercely desired and never realized. Because you didn't want it, but you couldn't say that and admit it to yourself. You couldn't say and admit to yourself that now your home was in Italy, was Italy. Not India, not anymore.

This sun, unwelcome guest, has made its way shamelessly into your Italian house, brightening and warming up everything in its path. Except for me. I don't play along. I avoid its light and warmth. I remain dark and cold, the way I feel, drenched in pain. I leave the kitchen. I move through the other rooms, and I see you walking. I follow you. You turn, you smile at me, you sit on the couch and pat the cushion.

You say, "Sit here, my child, next to me, and tell me how you're doing."

You hug me. I lean on your shoulder and fall on the armrest. It's ridiculous, what I'm doing. Seen from the outside, it might look like a comic sketch in a silent movie. Charlie Chaplin, for instance. Instead, it's your death and my life.

I open the bedroom door. I walk to the bed and run my fingers on the perfectly tightened and folded down sheets. I pull them down, crumple them, and toss them aside. That's what they were like when you slept here. I lie down and stare at the white ceiling with its plaster molding along the edges and a fan in the middle. I prop the pillows against the wall, sit up and remember when, in this same position, you would read *L'Unità* before going to sleep. And to my surprise, I see what you would see looking up from your newspaper. Before my eyes is a large painting, which I had never noticed: you had painted the four of us kids, playing in the sand and the water on the beach of Kovalam. Your brush stroke was soft and decisive. You used basic colors inflected in infinite shades. It's all blue and black, this canvas. Blue like the Indian Ocean and black like us, or perhaps blue and black like the flag of your beloved soccer team Inter. Maybe you weren't an artist, but it doesn't matter, painting was your hobby and not your profession. You didn't pursue fame, but rather pleasure. I live in pleasure while craving celebrity. I feel like an artist, and maybe I'm not one. Painting is my hobby, and I wish it were my profession. I'd like to be something that you weren't.

Maybe you weren't an artist, but you were definitely a soccer fan. Every Sunday you went to the stadium armed with horn, scarf, and cap. Meanwhile we, your children, shouted, "Go Milan! Go Milan!" — to which you replied, with an understanding smile: you have to kill your father to become an adult. It's better to kill him by destroying his favorite team than by destroying him. Your favorite team, by the way, was already destroying itself. So we had help. But we didn't expect to be hit like this in the counter-attack. We didn't expect that you'd die of your own accord. A heart attack!

What an unfair, unexpected play. A red card for sure, I'd say. You're no longer on the team now. And without the captain, it's hard to go on playing. Especially if memories clog up the present, blocking the future. Freezing everything in the here and now. Here where you were, now that you're no longer here.

I wish there were nothing left in this Italian house. I wish that furnishings and objects had vanished, that floors were polished and walls painted, so as to leave no trace of what it used to be. Of what you used to be. So that I'd no longer have a landscape where I can look for you. Maybe then I could come to cry for you over your grave.

My eyes have been dry since you've been gone. I haven't shed a single tear that might help me wash you away. And yet I have to search for you, and right here in this Italian house. I must rummage through your things to find the documents you talked to me about. I had told you I wanted them, and you brought them to me. They traveled with you from Trivandrum to Milan. Then I never asked you for them, and you never gave them to me. Maybe you were hurt. There it all was, your past. With my words, I told you it interested me, but with my actions, I ignored it. I'm trying to recoup, to make it up to you. *In extremis.* I turned your study upside down and finally found them. They were in a folder with my name written in block capitals. They are photocopies that have already turned yellow over time, and they are written in English and Malayalam. It's my fault I don't know English. You even told me, "Study it. It's important for your work." It's your fault I don't know Malayalam. I had told you, "Teach me. It's important for my life." I'm angry at myself and at you, now that I need a translator to read who you were. To learn your story and to fill mine with meaning.

I have a problem with split identity. I can't say that I'm half Indian if I know nothing about this half that belongs to me. If I have to look for it in writings I can't decipher.

I tore up everything. I tore up all of the documents you had brought me: those you had placed neatly in a folder with my name written in block capitals. I don't want to learn about you by filtering the information through a translator. I want to talk to you, sitting on the couch. While you hold me in your arms. I want to lean without falling. I want to understand why an Indian man loved to cook, got divorced, rooted for Inter, and wished for his only daughter not to depend on any man. Not even him. I want the tradition that was never passed down to me, not even through music or cooking. Bob Dylan and risotto Milanese? Give me a break. As if I were the daughter of some *brianzolo*[3] hippie. I want your past, the one you erased, in order to anchor myself in the present, where you no longer are. I want to be able to listen to a Hindu dirge while making *palak paneer*. I want to be able to say, "I'm half Indian," and feel that an echo of truth reverberates through my words.

I look at the torn-up papers, pull down the shades, lock the door, and find myself in the garden. Cherry and peach trees, no papaya or mango trees. It makes me blind and sweaty, this sun that didn't have the decency to leave out of respect for your absence and my presence. I would like to brush it away with my hand, and let the clouds in to paint the obscenely blue sky with white, gray, and black. And standing in stark contrast, the colors of your plants, which you cared for with the same love, always welcoming and never intrusive, that you had for your children. Jasmine, azaleas, roses, oleander, wisteria, bougainvillea, and daisies. And then the cherry and peach trees, of course. I would like to tear off their flowers and let their parched roots wither all the branches too.

I get in my car. I flee. I don't feel like looking for you anymore. Then I go back, get a spray can from the trunk, and draw graffiti on the wall. Is it defacement? Regardless, it's a gift from me. I left

3. Brianzolo: from Brianza, an affluent area in northwest Lombardy, between Milan and Lake Como. The area is close to Busto Arsizio, which is located 34 km northeast of Milan.

you something of mine. I gather my dreadlocks into a ponytail and turn on my portable CD player. In my ears the reggae bass syncs with my heartbeat, cancelling it out. And now where am I going to find you? In that acrylic painting on canvas, hanging on the wall in my living room. A dream never realized.

Amara Lakhous

A Premeditated Pregnancy[1]

I come out of the doctor's office a bit stunned. I feel like a drunk. My head is spinning. I sit down on the bus bench in Piazza Ippolito Nievo. I smile at people like a child. The trolley comes, but I don't get on. I'm still thinking about the doctor's words. I'm very happy. Who should I share my joy with? I call my parents, my sister Caterina, my cousin Silvia, then my partner Stefano. I can't hold back tears when I hear Stefano say, "Love, that's great! I'm overwhelmed." Everyone is happy.

Instead of going home, since I have a half-day off from work, I go back to the office in Largo Argentina. I don't understand why, perhaps I feel the need to have more people share my joy. I want to celebrate. I stop by the pastry shop and pick up a beautiful cake. At the café across from our agency, I ask for a bottle of *spumante*. I enter the office about four p.m. with the air of a Roman conqueror. My four colleagues look at me, puzzled.

"Ilaria! Why are you back?" says Sandra, the most anxious of the group. Then Carlo's ironic comment follows promptly, "Ilaria, did your American uncle finally show up? Or have you hit the lottery jackpot?" Alessia and Barbara instead remain silent, impatient to know what's going on. I let a few seconds go by to add to the suspense before making the big announcement: "I'm pregnant!" And away we go with jumps of joy, kisses and hugs! My colleagues' happiness is sincere. We're a small family. I've been working for this real estate agency for five years. There have been years of temporary employment and so many sacrifices. I was only hired on a permanent basis six months ago. An important

1. Amara Lakhous, "Una gravidanza premeditata," *La Repubblica,* October 19, 2008.

milestone. Then my life took another turn: after years of being engaged to Stefano, we began talking about marriage, about applying for a mortgage, about having children. Let's face it: we aren't kids anymore, as my mother says when she sees me going out with him on Saturday night. She's right: he's 39 and I'm 36! My colleagues compete to propose both boy and girl names for the new arrival. So many beautiful names, and others to be avoided, such as Assunta and Gianmaria, to name a few. As far as I'm concerned, the question of names has been closed for years: Paolo if it's a boy, Francesca if it's a girl.

There's no shortage of advice and recommendations on childbirth. The women are divided between delivery by epidural and water birth. The important thing is to avoid pain and suffering. It's 2008 and science has made a lot of progress. In other words, women should stop suffering. For the moment I'm not thinking about childbirth — there's time. However, I pretend to be interested in what they're telling me, although my mind is elsewhere.

"What's going on here?" It's the boss, Dr. Castellani, the owner of the agency.

Barbara's response is prompt: "We're celebrating a big event." Barbara likes prefaces and long introductions. The boss, no. So it's Sandra who as usual saves the boat from shipwreck: "Doctor Castellani, Ilaria's going to be a mother!"

"Congratulations," he replies.

"Doctor," says Carlo, "have a drink. Come and celebrate with us."

"No thanks," he responds. And going into his office he adds, "Ilaria, can you come into my office please?"

I follow him, carrying with me my glass of *spumante*. After closing the door, he looks at me: "Is this story about a pregnancy true?"

"Yes."

"Then it's a premeditated pregnancy."

"Premeditated pregnancy? I'm sorry, sir, I don't understand."

"Come on, Ilaria, don't be smart with me. You waited to have a permanent contract before getting pregnant. Isn't that right? Congratulations on your plan."

"But what plan, sir?..."

"You betrayed my trust. This is a stab in the back. You know that the agency is going through a delicate period. The mortgage crisis in America is approaching like a tornado. Did you think about the agency? When you go on maternity leave, what am I supposed to do? Hire another person? There will be expenses...."

"I'll speak with my colleagues right now, we'll find a solution for replacing me. I'm willing to give up my holidays and..."

"Look, Ilaria, I was really counting on you. A trusting relationship is fundamental in our work. Unfortunately, you've deeply disappointed me. This is betrayal."

"Betrayal? I'm only pregnant by my partner!"

"Yes, it's a professional betrayal. Because of you, the agency will suffer very serious consequences. The market is in an uproar. We have to be competitive!"

"I haven't betrayed anyone!"

"Don't cry now. Let's try to fix this. Can't you put off this pregnancy until the subprime mortgage crisis is over?"

"What does the mortgage crisis have to do with this, sir?"

"Ilaria, listen to me, this is not the time to be playing mommy! The agency is going through a rough time. Don't you understand?"

"You are asking me to have an abortion, sir."

"Ilaria, you're still young. These days the fertility period of women is longer. You can even have children at fifty."

"It's my right to have a child."

"No one is saying otherwise. However, there are priorities. I have an agency to look after. It's just a matter of putting it off for a year or two. So it's up to you to choose."

"Choose?"

"Yes, choose between your pregnancy and your job."

"I have to choose between my pregnancy and my job?"

"Exactly. Now you must excuse me. I have a job to finish."

I leave the boss's office with my face streaming with tears. It's not easy to pass from the stars to the pits! I don't have to explain to my colleagues what's happened. They understood right away. Someone offers to accompany me home. But I refuse. I want to be alone. I decide to walk back home to Piazza della Radio.

The boss's words are still ringing in my ears: premeditated pregnancy, professional betrayal, the mortgage crisis, and so on. I'm confused. The flow of thoughts and memories doesn't stop. I try to understand my boss's disappointment. I remember some theories of Annalisa, a friend of mine from college, on women in the workplace. She maintained that men have no respect for their female colleagues because they consider them unfair competitors. Women in the workplace always have an extra weapon: sexual capital. Because of this, women are divided into three categories: those who have already used it, those who are about to use it, and lastly, those who will use it later.

It's just a question of sex, and nothing else. That's what our male colleagues think of us! But perhaps the boss had some sexual expectations concerning me that I wasn't aware of? Was hiring me just an advance on a service to be rendered?

My head is exploding.

While I try desperately to understand that damn "professional betrayal," I get a text from my sister's friend: "Congratulations, you're expecting! Enjoy the joyous anticipation!" Sorry, honey, there won't be any joyous anticipation. I have to decide right away if I should keep my baby or my job. Assuming I choose not to abort, because that's what it's about, there are other problems to consider: how to reconcile my role of working woman with that of mother? Unfortunately, I can't count on help from my parents. They are drowning in their own health problems — no way they'd be able to take care of a baby. Not to mention daycare. The waiting lists are very long. It takes a miracle and a lot of connections to enter the rankings! Raising a child today is no joke. I was reading the other day in a newspaper that the cost of supporting a child until age eighteen is somewhere around three hundred thousand Euros. That's the price of a house in Rome. I can't allow myself the luxury of being unemployed now. Of course, I can always sue, but I don't trust Italian justice. How long will the case last? Will the verdict be in my favor? Will I receive compensation? Will I be reintegrated into my job? The truth is I no longer have any trust in this society. I've done my part. I graduated from college. I completed a few Masters programs and a multitude of training courses. Stefano gets along as best he can. He racks up annual contracts and many hiring promises. We can't go on this way. Starting a family is truly a far-off dream. Unfortunately we should have emigrated years ago. It's a little late now. I read another text, from my Aunt Gabriella: "Dear Ilaria, being a mother is a gift from God. You're very lucky. Congratulations and may you have many sons!"[2]

Lucky? Me? Give me a break. I have to choose between two destinies: unemployed mama or working woman wounded and humiliated in her womanhood. Unfortunately, my "premeditated" pregnancy will certainly not be a time of joyous anticipation. What will become of me?

2. *Figli maschi* ("male children"), the traditional Italian wish for expectant parents, is a remnant of times past when male children were considered greater assets to a family than their "weaker" siblings. The sons, of course, would also carry on the family name.

Tahar Lamri

Preface[1]

Let me start by saying that I am neither a literary theorist nor a literary critic. What I'm going to speak to you about now concerns my efforts to write in Italian, the tortures that rule that decision, and some general reflections of mine on migrant writing in Italy, determined more by "feelings" than by scientific analysis.

For me, writing in Italy, the country in which I have chosen to live, and co-exist, living in the Italian language, living with it and making it coexist with my other maternal languages (the Algerian dialect, Arabic, and in a certain sense, French) means perhaps creating in some way the illusion of having put down roots there. Mangrove roots, on the surface, always on the borderline that separates the fresh water of memory from the salt water of everyday life.

Consequently, for me writing does not represent mere nomadism, in search of literary pastures, but rather a circular pilgrimage not lacking in bewilderment, looting, wonder, myth, and perhaps the return to self. By which I mean endlessly losing my own identity, and cultivating in secret, like the Marranos of Spain during the Reconquista, my primordial identity in a place beyond wandering. Perhaps it is a search for the *anima plurima* with its pagan implications. Writing in a foreign language is a pagan act, because if the mother tongue protects, the foreign tongue desecrates and liberates.

---

1. This preface and the following three short stories by Tahar Lamri — "Fragile come carne nuda," "20 Kg (e) di datteri," and "La convivialità delle differenze" — are from *I sessanta nomi dell'amore* (Naples: Michele Di Salvo Editore, 2007).

But can the illusion of primordial identity be cultivated in a language that is already foreign? In a language that still echoes with my early stammering? So short is the time period spent in efforts to learn to speak it, even roughly, in order to exit my post-diluvian Macondo, composed of nameless objects. So short the space of time spent in advancing my desire to use this same language to describe my deepest feelings, with words laid down, aligned on several rows, but in a state of constant wakefulness, that speak to the imagination of others. At times even snatching with both hands from the rough dialects of the plains. Don't you think that's asking for a lot?

I've lived in Romagna since 1987, ever since I've been in Italy. In this region, especially among the elderly, the most affectionate form of greeting is "Drop dead!"

I remember in 2002, during the Azioni in Clementi Festival in Malo, I was outside Villa Clementi, waiting to take part in a discussion about migration literature. Near me were two locals, who were reading the program for the day. One asked the other to explain an item in the program, and the other replied *"Ze una roba di cultura!"*[2] These are the things that fascinate me and compel me to write. I would like to push my migrant experience to embrace dialects and from there to construct the Italian language together with Italian writers. A new language that might allow me, even while carrying along with me my native culture and the cultures that have influenced me through all these years of journey (Libya, Egypt, France, Switzerland, Poland, England, India), to finally complete the Voyage — with a capital V — of visibility along with other Italian writers. Beyond the realm of classic Italian literature, however, since my school studies were not nurtured by Manzoni's *I Promessi Sposi* or by the poems of Pascoli, an experience that verges on a primordial reconciliation. And perhaps it is no accident that in my case, the text I read and re-read most often is "The Song of Solomon."

2. Veneto slang: "It's that culture stuff."

Fragile as Naked Flesh

Under the probing blue lights of the high ceiling in that hospital ward, Zidane, whose tall and emaciated body resembles a kind of wild asparagus, was even more curved in upon himself than usual. He raised his gaze and looked toward the window. He saw heavy round drops of rain, like an ancient omen, that obscured a far-off bell tower. He sighed. He was cold. He walked along the corridor looking down at the tips of his shoes. He saw the reflection of the ceiling lights streaming along the polished floor. He went back to the window and saw himself multiplied in the glass and darkness of the storm. He looked foreign and aged. On the window he saw one drop of rain capture others, creating changeable and meaningless torrents. He suddenly remembered his panic of yesterday when the unexpected made the convictions of a lifetime falter.

"Ah, hi, Zidane...you're here!"

Zidane smiled without opening his lips and said, "Hi, Carlo."

He gazed at the city sparkling with rain within the embrace of the dusk that was falling in that moment.

"How's the boy?" murmured Carlo.

"Fine. Better. Decidedly better," Zidane responded with difficulty.

"We were lucky. Thank goodness the ambulance arrived quickly...."

"The boy is fine, but I'm a mess," Zidane interrupted.

"It's perfectly understandable! You know I'm here for you. You can count on me...."

"Perhaps you didn't understand,..." Zidane observed a moment of silence. Carlo stroked his arm and put his hand on Zidane's shoulder until he continued:

"You know, by 'a mess' I mean that my life will never be the same as before."

He smiled with his eyes and then went on: "Before, I thought that being modern, integrated, free, meant leaving behind both religious traditions and all the others I considered crap. But now, what happened has shaken my convictions to the core, and I see that life requires balance." Zidane looked around for something to hold on to, but the unadorned ward offered only walls painted halfway with gray. He looked at the tips of his fingers, then continued: "Don't you get it? At the table we always joked about this. My son would say, 'Come on, taste a little salami. You don't know what you're missing' and stuff like that. But when I saw him with blue lips, and I realized that a piece of prosciutto stood between him and me, could take him away from me forever.... In that instant, I, who considered myself non-religious, if not an atheist — I thought for an instant that it was a punishment or a divine warning. Do you understand what I'm trying to say?"

"I understand," Carlo said. "The son of a Muslim choking on a piece of prosciutto, isn't exactly...." Carlo couldn't hold back a laugh, resonant as the raindrops earlier. Even Zidane laughed silently with his belly shaking, while outside, night blurred the outlines of the city and the window sent the image of bodies convulsed with laughter back into infinity.

TWENTY KG (℮) OF DATES[3]

Today is Thursday, in a month that had proven rainy from the start. Getting off the plane at the Bologna airport, no sweet smells greet me, my hands touch only the cold railing of the gangway. No one is waiting for me. The asphalt of the runway is a smooth and solid black, as are all the faces around me. None of them look familiar to me. Strangely, my footsteps are not uncertain.

The trip from the airport to the city is as short as it is lonely. I'm the only passenger on a shuttle for those who can't afford a taxi and who have no one waiting for them at the airport.

I retrieve my luggage, consisting of only a backpack, and head down to the train station. My backpack is heavy. I don't know why, but instead of wearing it on my shoulders, I hold it in my hand as if it were a carryall. The predominant red of the city buildings hits me like a slap in the face. Uncertain, I don't know if I should enter the train station or set out for the downtown area, which I see indicated by a sign with three concentric circles. There ahead of me, like an omen, is some kind of garden, full of homeless people. I turn my gaze elsewhere. Everything seems clean, neat, and orderly. I'll come to learn that the natives don't see railroad stations the same way. The heavy automobile traffic on the avenue in front irresistibly attracts me. I decide to go downtown, partly to see what it looks like, but also because I've been told that's where the Caritas Center is located, where no one is ever denied a bowl of pasta. I might have taken maybe two steps when that police officer yanked the backpack from my hands and spilled the contents onto the ground. Twenty kilos of dates.

---

3. The original title is "20 Kg (℮) di datteri"; the symbol ℮ is the "estimated" sign or e-mark that can be found on some prepackaged goods sold within the European Union. It indicates that the packaging is in accordance with European Union Directive, and complies with specific average requirements allowing a limited negative margin of error between stated and actual weights.

The Conviviality of Differences

Milan, 10:30 p.m. It had been a rather exhausting day what with the late trains. And besides, for those who have to travel, leaving Ravenna by any mode of transportation is always tiring. It's probably because of the Via Emilia. Who knows.

For more than an hour this Professor Antonio Pasini has been yammering about multiculturalism, interculturalism, melting pots, and things like that. I can't stand listening to these talks any more. In fact, it seems to me that this gentleman has only known foreigners through the books he has written. Himself!

I'm so fed up with these talks that I feel like taking notes. He's saying, "Italy today is experiencing a reversed migration flow. From the post-war period to the present it has welcomed many non-EU peoples in various waves." Boy, am I sleepy. I wasn't able to sleep on the train thanks to that lady who at all costs wanted to hear my "nice" accent. Her word exactly.

Pasini is talking on and on and on: "Changes in culture from monoculture to the plurality of cultures…goal…interculture.…" What a drag! Since when has Italy, in the course of its history, ever been monocultural. Think about it: someone from Pantelleria with someone from Tarvisio or from Ayas-Champoluc.

I'm thinking about a guy from Romagna forced to eat mustard with his *Bollito Misto*. "An atrocity!" he would say. He'd think he had been suddenly plunged into a foreign land. And then yesterday, Roberto, a guy who works with the Arci Association[4]

4. The Associazione Ricreativa Culturale Italiana (Italian Cultural and Recreational Association) is the largest non-profit organization in Italy not affiliated with the Roman Catholic Church. Founded in Florence in 1957, it united thousands of local groups already operating all over Italy for the aid and benefit of Italian workers.

spoke to me at length about Naples and a surprising tradition that filled my heart with joy. He said, "Do you know what 'pay-it-forward' is?" No, I didn't know about that. "Pay-it-forward," Roberto told me, "is when in Naples someone wakes up in a good mood, goes to the café, orders their own breakfast and then pays for another one — it might be a cup of coffee, a complete meal, any kind of beverage — for someone who comes later. When I was a student, I used to go into the café and ask, 'Is there anything paid-forward?' and frequently there were several 'paid-forwards,' so I could take my pick, and for years I got by thanks to the good nature of other Neapolitans." Monoculture. When has Italy ever been monocultural. I'd like to see someone from Milan or Turin pay something forward. When Pasini pays something forward in a coffee shop in northern Italy and the barista doesn't pocket the money, then we can talk about solidarity and all these things that are now confined to conferences. Just so you know. And then of course Roberto and I also talked about music. We spoke of Concetta and Peppe Barra, and Sicilian Rosa Balistreri. And who has ever heard of them in the rest of Italy?

Pasini talks from his pulpit but doesn't pay any attention to me, a foreigner. He likes his theories about me better than me in person. He's talking about the redefinition of one's own identity and of the changed sociocultural context. Where this context has changed, I don't know. Maybe because there are more colored faces. What a change!

Look, I can't stand it any more and in order to play Mr. Contrary (can you say that?), you know what I say? Foreigners are not necessarily pursuing an intercultural goal. Foreigners identify with what truly integrates, and you know what that is? The consumption model. The one you believe is depersonalizing and alienating. Never mind the conviviality of differences! Now I'm formulating theories too? Perhaps. But at least they are mine, and they concern me.

Oh! He's done. Now it's my turn. I really must be less bitter. My talk must be balanced, otherwise how will we ever build this new society?

Geneviève Makaping

Anthropological Journey of a Bamiléké Immigrant[1]

"I want to marry you, I've been watching you since I got here. I like you a lot."

For more than a month Marcel had been staying at Père Takala's hotel, the Hotel des Palmiers. He was with a friend of his. They had come from another African country, Gabon — so they said. Marcel had been watching me for a long time. Among my people, observation is not so direct, especially when it comes to asking for a woman's hand in marriage. It's the parents, the closest relatives, or trusted friends who do the observing on behalf of the interested party.

I would never have thought that observation would come back into my life with such powerful impact, that I'd have a job where observation is fundamental. Only many years after coming to the West did I discover that scientists base their research on observation.

At home, we used to go to the movies every Saturday. I had heard that kind of declaration in romantic movies. We also saw a lot of Westerns and movies from India. In the ones from India, we liked the charm, the singing, and the pain of the women in love. We were more struck by the Westerns. The Indians were the bad guys, and they were wiped out. Blacks seemed to have better luck: they served and said "yes, master," keeping their eyes down, and they laughed loudly (he he he). To us, they didn't "signify."

1. "Il viaggio antropologico di un'immigrata Bamiléké" and the other two pieces by Geneviève Makaping — "L'osservazione partecipante di un soggetto eccentrico: Una riflessione," and "In treno. Pordenone-Verona" — are from *Traiettorie di sguardi. E se gli altri foste voi?* (Trajectory of Gazes: What If the Others Were You?) (Soveria Mannelli (CZ): Rubbettino, 2001).

Us girls and boys from my neighborhood, from my city (I'd soon extend this generalization to a large number of Africans), we identified with the whites. We imitated the laughter (ha ha ha ha!) of the winners in the Westerns. We cheered for them against the Indians and insulted the Indians from our seats. The whites never cried. They didn't get sick and didn't complain. For us, it was all real. We had never heard of cinematographic fiction. The whites were beautiful and rich. Most importantly, they were white, and that was enough. Among us, to say that people were beautiful, rich, good, well mannered, and all the best you could say about them, it was enough to say that they were white, *"c'est un blanc, c'est une blanche."* If one of us emigrated and had the least bit of success, we said *"c'est notre blanc,"* he is our white. Whiteness had significance. Even for the girls. When their parents were asked for their hands in marriage, the lighter their complexion, the higher their value as brides. Skin color that was too dark devalued or trivialized the merchandise. "Black like coal" is an expression we use to show contempt. Our attitude toward the whites was "active envy." We didn't want to be "them." We wanted to have what "they" had. We wanted to do what "they" did. Only later, when whitening products arrived from America and France, would a lot of women and some young men opt to change the color of their skin. I tried it myself, too, and burned my skin. I was fourteen. Out of shame, I didn't leave the house.

The Participant Observation of an Eccentric[2] Subject: A Reflection

These observation exercises that I am doing as an "ethnologist" haven't met with much popularity. For me, at this point, it's a challenge, a gamble. The people, educated people, I spoke to about my initiative, seem to be very annoyed, almost upset. I have to resort to — forgive me — a strong image to express my feelings. It's as if I had used their bathroom after a week of constipation and had forgotten to flush. The truth is that, in reality, I'm not challenging any of *them.* The true challenge is to myself, to relate in the first person the things I've seen, understood, lived, experienced, at times painfully, in the flesh. They're minor acts of abuse and violence that, all together, can become public harassment. Not for me. I'm at peace. I'm at peace and disheartened. My skin is still here, with me.

Instead, the skin of many victims of so-called "clichés" has already been buried by virtue of their presumed "otherness." But which of the two is the "other," the victim or the executioner? I truly hope, at this point, to be able to continue this "journey," thanks to my encounter with Professor Tabet. The conscious choice of non-violence is also painful. The only advantage of this choice, and it's no small thing, is that when you get up in the morning, even after a sleepless night, your conscience is clear. I'm greatly tormented by injustice, but I have inner peace. If I had full command of the language, I could even discuss this statement at length. Sadly, I don't — neither in Italian, nor in Cameroonian Bahuanese, nor in English — even though these are all languages in which I express myself. None of them, however, has taken

2. *Eccèntrico* adj. (m. pl. -ci). *1.* Not having the same center; *esp.* said of two circles, one containing the other, whose centers do not coincide / *broad.* distant from the center [. . .]; *2. fig.* Bizarre, extravagant (G. Devoto, G.C. Oli, *Dizionario della lingua italiana,* Florence: Le Monnier). [AN]

possession of me, nor I of them. Believe me, it's no contradiction. The reason for my peace of mind may be interpreted from various points of view. From my standpoint, it depends on my deep love for Jesus Christ....

The more I write this diary, the more questions I ask myself: why should I have to defend the color of my skin? Why do some people have to "justify" being an outsider?[3] Their extraneousness? Being foreigners? And yet I know very well that the problem isn't skin color, which, in the obvious cases, is only the tip of the iceberg.

If my premise wasn't a purely ethnological investigation, then I wonder, what am I doing, why am I observing? I find the answer in my *eccentric* position. Choosing to place oneself in a particular position doesn't always happen automatically, let alone naturally. The point is, it was the *others* who put me at the margins, and I subsequently chose to locate myself there, in order to make my own choices. Recognizing myself in the theoretical and pragmatic position of an *eccentric subject* wasn't easy.... I was afraid that claiming my "eccentricity" might legitimize the thinking of those who believe that I am "bound" to see things in these terms: "She can't read things any other way because she considers herself to be victimized...persecuted."

Am I prejudiced? Perhaps. But it's important to allow a margin of error until one finds confirmation. I have lived in the West for half of my life, and I know its preconceptions, the ones that take away and negate the individuality of those who are *other than us.* I want to be able to choose, think, and act without preconceptions, and to do that, one must have the tools to "unlearn" them. One must "educate" oneself to eliminate prejudice.

3. In the original, "extra-comunitarietà" indicates specifically the condition of being outside of the EU, a non-EU citizen.

ON THE TRAIN. PORDENONE-VERONA

At a midway station, a black woman climbs aboard. There are many empty seats. She sits opposite me, by the window. She is from Ghana. At a later station, many people board the train. I remove my purse from the vacant seat next to me. "No, no, leave it there, you know none of them will come to sit near to us anyway." Sure enough, nobody came over to sit near us. Along the way to her destination, we formed the "tribe" of "us" (black women, immigrants, different, possibly even prostitutes, non EU-citizens), carefully avoided by the "others," almost all of them young people. Their attitude no longer leaves me indifferent. It makes me feel bad, and I get angry. I get angry about the "circumstances" that make these young people instinctively "excrete racism through their pores." They show disgust, not for my way of thinking, which might conceivably be the same as theirs, but for my appearance, which is an "incident,"[4] pure "chance," the same as their own skin, hair, eyes, etc.... It makes me feel bad, but I try to engage in dialogue anyway, because listening is my priority, even more than understanding. *They,* all around me, are my observation "material," and I am inside "the field." If it weren't for the bitterness that at times results from my observations, I'd even be amused by the fact that people don't know I'm watching them. They are spontaneous, and therefore "cooperate." All the way to our destination, nobody took a seat next to "us."

4. In English in the original text.

Ndjock Ngana

L'Africano[1]

Scendo dal raggio di sole,
sgorgo dalla roccia solida,
parlo la lingua della vita,
ed emano odio ed amore.
Lasciatemi vivere.

Dov'è la mia storia,
la vostra storia, nostra storia?

Cerco la pace,
compagna del passato,
utopia del presente,
sogno del futuro,
sogno, semplice sogno.
Lasciatemi sognare.

Dove sono gli eroi della mia terra?
Voglio sapere ciò che è nascosto
per ritrovare me stesso.
Lasciatemi indagare.

Non sono miei quelli che sono caduti
per i propri interessi,
o per aiutare l'impostore;
rivoglio i miei caduti
per onorarli.

---

1. This selection of poems is from Ndjock Ngana's collection *Ñhindô / Nero. Poesie in lingua Basaa e in lingua italiana* (Rome: Kel'Lam, 1999). They were fist published in *Foglie vive calpestate: Riflessioni sotto il Baobab* (Rome: UCSEI, 1989). The versions included in this anthology were provided by the author.

The African

I come down from a ray of sunshine,
I flow out of solid rock,
I speak the language of life,
and I exude both hate and love.
          Let me live.

Where is my story,
your story, our story?

I am looking for peace,
companion of bygone times,
present-day utopia,
dream of the future;
a dream, a simple dream.
          Let me dream.

Where are my country's heroes?
I want to find what is hidden
in order to rediscover myself.
          Let me investigate.

I disown those who fell
in the pursuit of self-interest,
or in support of an impostor;
I want to reclaim my fallen
to honor them.

Percorro una via ignota
perché un involucro
mi ricopre l'anima.
Dove sono i miei preti?
I miei intellettuali?
La mia anima?
La mia strada?

Voglio una prospettiva di libertà
anche per me.

Il sangue

Chi può versare
sangue nero
sangue giallo
sangue bianco
mezzo sangue?

Il sangue non è indio, polinesiano o inglese.

Nessuno ha mai visto
sangue ebreo,
sangue cristiano,
sangue musulmano,
sangue buddista.

Il sangue non è ricco, povero o benestante.

Il sangue è rosso!

Disumano è chi lo versa
ma non chi lo porta.

I travel an unknown path
because a shell
covers my soul.
Where are my priests?
My intellectuals?
My soul?
My road?

I want the prospect of freedom
for myself, too.

Blood

Who can spill
black blood
yellow blood
white blood
half blood?

Blood isn't Indian, Polynesian or English.

No one has ever seen
Jewish blood,
Christian blood,
Muslim blood,
Buddhist blood.

Blood isn't rich, poor or comfortably off.

Blood is red!

Inhuman are those who spill it,
not those who carry it.

Prigione

Vivere una sola vita,
in una sola città,
in un solo Paese,
in un solo universo,
vivere in un solo mondo
è prigione.

Amare un solo amico,
un solo padre,
una sola madre,
una sola famiglia,
amare una sola persona
è prigione.

Conoscere una sola lingua,
un solo lavoro,
un solo costume,
una sola civiltà,
conoscere una sola logica
è prigione.

Avere un solo corpo,
un solo pensiero,
una sola conoscenza,
una sola essenza,
avere un solo essere
è prigione.

Prison

Living only one life,
    in one city,
    in one country,
    in one universe,
living in only one world
is prison.

Loving only one friend,
    one father,
    one mother,
    one family,
loving only one person
is prison.

Knowing only one language,
    one job,
    one way of life,
    one civilization,
knowing only one way of thinking
is prison.

Having only one body,
    one thought,
    one understanding,
    one essence,
having only one existence
is prison.

Jarmila Očkayová

Eye on Pinocchio[1]

Chapter 1

My name is Pinocchio, and I want to tell you my story. Tell it from my point of view. Oh, I can imagine what you're thinking, and I feel one thing needs to be made clear right away: mine isn't a case of antonomasia, let alone the case of a wily epigone who wants to exploit someone else's fame. Let me make it crystal clear: I *am* Pinocchio. *That* Pinocchio, yes.

I know, you all know my story. The one written more than a century ago by Carlo Lorenzini.

Collodi, to be clear.

So what more is there to add?

Perhaps not much to add, but a lot to remove. Collodi told my story the way a story is told to children, by choosing to say certain things and omit others. He told it the way one carves a wooden statue, a puppet if you will, by taking off the superfluous. Children know this very well: that every story is ready-made and to tell it, you just have to uncover it, remove the layers and the build-up that hide it. Children listen and understand, and the story that Collodi told about me was perfect for being listened to and understood. But then grown-ups took that story into their own hands — and my troubles began, because grown-ups do not listen. They want to be listened to. They don't understand. They want to make you understand. Not "make themselves understood," mind you. Make

1. From Jarmila Očkayová's novel *Occhio a Pinocchio* (Isernia: Cosmo Iannone, 2006).

you understand! Where a carpenter or a sculptor removes in order to give shape, grown-ups add in order to explain that same shape. And it's as if they were taking an already carved figure and gluing back on all the discarded wood chips. And then they actually stand there, admiring their collage of chips and shavings, convinced that they've mastered the mystery of the word.... They've been playing this game with me for one hundred twenty-five years. For one hundred twenty-five years, they've been adding and adding, and now I look more like a stuffed scarecrow than a puppet. Piece by piece, patch by patch, from patching to mending, from undershirts of outworn theories to jackets of discarded symbols. By now they've stuck anything and everything on me. And at this point I can surely say that even a puppet's patience has its limits. One hundred twenty-five years of patience seems like enough to me, and I dare anyone to disagree.

So now the time has come to dot the famous i's. As I was saying earlier, it's time to tell my story from my point of view. The point of view of a puppet without strings.

It won't be simple, and I'm aware of this. Because this is precisely what grown-ups fear: a puppet's point of view. This is why they've been going after me for so long. They know perfectly well — the grown-ups — that deep down I remain always and forever a wooden puppet, even though, at the end of Collodi's story, I become a fine, flesh-and-blood boy. If they could really believe in that metamorphosis, they'd leave me alone: flesh-and-blood children grow up and are afraid and need a thousand things, and a thousand more needs and fears can be invented just for them along the way, until they're all covered with wrinkles and oblivion. But a puppet like me, a puppet without strings, is something terrible for grown-ups. Terrible because it's uncontrollable. It's like having to face the very essence of a tree, with its roots firmly anchored in the ground and its branches freely reaching for the sky. And with its breath that breathes life into you and takes your breath away for the impenetrable simplicity of that mystery that every tree is: an axis between sky and earth.

An axis between sky and earth: a straight line without any zigzags, negotiations, red triangles indicating the right of way, or required stops. A tree is an invitation to lift your head and look up, that's all. And that's precisely all it takes, or would take, to throw grown-ups into a panic. Moving from the vertical to the horizontal plane, it's as if humankind discovered that it's possible to do without the invention of the telephone, or handle it with complete autonomy: click with your finger in the air and you'll connect with whomever you want — maybe a Chinese who's crossing Tiananmen Square in Beijing, to have him tell you about life beyond the Great Wall. From phone companies to newscast directors, the entire telecommunication system would break down.

This is what Collodi had in mind when he called me Pinocchio: pine-eye. The eye of a tree. Even if, more than the eye, we puppets without strings represent the heart of a tree. But that's just a small detail, a shortcut taken by your lexicon and your way of perceiving the world. Because in a tree, the eye and the heart are one and the same.

Even the story of Master Cherry — who supposedly gave Geppetto the block of firewood from which I would be carved — is nothing but a shortcut. In reality Geppetto and I met in the woods.

I was still a branch, a natural appendage on the trunk of my tree. And yet, in my shape, I already vaguely resembled a boy's body. Not by chance: some time before Geppetto arrived — maybe a few decades, figuring by your time coordinates — a little boy climbed up my tree and wrapped himself right around me, and for a few minutes there was such a perfect symbiosis between us that something of him penetrated under my bark and infiltrated my lymph and vascular tissue. Geppetto noticed it right away, which is why he stopped right by me. He saw me as I would become.

To translate it into your language, you might say: he got the idea of carving a puppet.

In Geppetto's House, from Chapter 5

In short, in that house I was happy. In that house, I knew harmony — the harmony that humans can achieve, and without any false note, I might say — were it not for the memory of one small fact, one really tiny little fact, which, however, always caused me a faint unease.

The fact has to do with the issue of Geppetto's mirror. When, a few days after my arrival, I decided to look myself in the face, to finally see its reflection, I tried several times. I planted myself in front of the mirror and stepped sideways and leaned down and rose up on my toes. . .in short, I did a lot of bending and stretching and twisting to try to avoid a certain dark spot that prevented me from seeing my reflection, but I kept finding it in front of me. It was always there, making my face look like a summer-storm cloud.

At first it didn't bother me that much. My curiosity was fickle and in any case it was distracted and engrossed by a thousand other things that I was discovering by being near Geppetto. But then, with time, it became a sort of obsession, and between one distraction and another, I'd run to the mirror constantly to make an umpteenth attempt. Of course Geppetto immediately noticed my discombobulation, but didn't talk about it. Until the day when I blurted out in exasperation: "But what do I have to do to be able to look at my own face?!"

Then he calmly replied: "You have to pull out your soul."

"And how do I do that?"

"I'll tell you tomorrow."

The following day Geppetto left home early and came back with the famous A-B-C book. He put it in my hands and said: "Start here."

"Is my soul in here?"

"No, the alphabet is in here."

"And my soul is in the alphabet?"

"The world is in the alphabet. And so are you."

"And my soul?"

"To draw water from the well you need a bucket and a pulley. To open a locked door you need a key and a hand to turn it. To…"

"All right, all right, I get it! But it's not fair."

"What's not fair?"

"That all the others can start by looking at their own faces, and instead I have to go though all this.…"

"And are you absolutely sure that all the others see their own faces in the mirror?"

"At least they don't see a dark spot!"

"I repeat: are you absolutely sure?"

Geppetto was like that. When he was supposed to be giving me answers, he would start asking a bunch of questions.

And so it was that I left to go to school. Very happy I was to go there, since I knew — as everyone else knows — that in school, before asking you a question, they give you the answer. They put it in front of you, ready and waiting, and all you have to do, later, when they start asking questions, is repeat it. And the more exactly you repeat it — just the way they told you it — the more they appreciate you. And I wanted answers, and I wanted to be appreciated. I was as fed up with the dark spots on the mirror as I was with Geppetto's riddles.

Candelaria Romero

Immigrata senza voto[1]

Mi aggiro rotonda
nella città quadrata
spigoli arrestano il fiato
riconosco che non vuoi vedermi
non vuoi baciarmi
no mirarme *no* besarme
invece baciami
besame mucho
per quello che sono
per quello che tu non sei in me.

---

1. Candelaria Romero, *Poesie di fine mondo* (Falloppio (CO): LietoColle, 2010).

Immigrant without a Vote

Round I wander
in the square city
sharp corners take my breath away
I recognize that you don't want to see me
don't want to kiss me
no *mirarme* no *besarme*
but do kiss me
besame mucho
for what I am
for what you are not in me.

La colf[2]

Corteo studentesco blocca il traffico
manifestanti sbandierano a ritmo di musica ska
dalle finestre della CGIL sindacalisti piangono.

Dentro attillati pantaloni tigrati
la colf attraversa la strada
arriccia il naso scuro
impreca in swahili
arriverà tardi dal padrone.
Antichi diritti dipinti a mano.

Giornata dei fuori luogo[3]

Come nell'antico carnevale oggi le parti s'invertono
ciò che ieri usciva sconnesso
oggi danza composto.
La matta del panificio sorride prontamente
sa cosa voglio
sicura mi augura buon pomeriggio
ringrazio perplessa e felice
oggi è il nostro giorno.

2. Romero, *Poesie di fine mondo.*
3. Romero, *Poesie di fine mondo.*

The Cleaning Lady

A student demonstration blocks traffic
protesters wave flags to the beat of ska[1]
from the windows of CGIL[2] headquarters trade unionists weep.

Clad in tight tiger-print pants
the cleaning lady crosses the street
wrinkling her dark nose
cursing in Swahili
she'll get to her boss's late for work.
Ancient rights, hand painted.

Day of the Out of Place

As in the ancient carnival, today roles are reversed
what yesterday came out disjointed
dances composedly today.
The madwoman at the bakery flashes a smile
she knows what I want
confident she wishes me good day
puzzled and happy, I thank her
today is our day.

---

1. Ska is a musical genre that originated in Jamaica in the late 1950s. Precursor of Rocksteady and Reggae, it combines elements of Carribean Mento and Calipso with American Jazz and Rhythm and Blues.

2. CGIL stands for Confederazione Generale Italiana del Lavoro (Italian General Confederation of Labor), the most important Italian trade union since its creation, in 1944, by agreement between Socialists, Communists, and Christian Democrats.

Landscape e inscape[4]

a Mia, amica migrante

Un paesaggio fuori ed un altro dentro
i colori non coincidono
tra le fughe della tavolozza ci si perde
l'aria diventa piccola
risposte stringono.
Raccogliamo cartoline turistiche
viaggi del non ritorno.

Per Pollicina[5]

Desidero per te un abbraccio
pelle che avvolge.

Desidero per te sospiri di sangue
che portino profumi fertili.

Desidero per te una coperta di aliti
un cuscino di guancia
e che tutto questo abbia un inizio e una fine quotidiana.

Desidero per te terra
umida e calpestata
ovunque tu vada.

---

4. Romero, *Poesie di fine mondo.*

5. Romero, *Salto mortale* (Falloppio (CO): LietoColle, 2014).

Landscape and Inscape

to Mia, migrant friend

One landscape outside and another inside
the colors don't match
we get lost in the flights of the palette
the air gets small
answers get tight.
We collect tourist postcards
journeys of no return.

For Thumbelina

I wish you an embrace
skin that envelops you

I wish you sighs of blood
carrying fertile scents.

I wish you a blanket of breaths
a cheek for a pillow
and that all this may have a beginning and an end each day.

I wish you earth
moist and trodden
everywhere you go.

Ci vorrebbe un'invenzione[6]

Ci vorrebbe un'invenzione
per accorciare distanze
la strada giusta nel cielo
la luna nata con l'acqua.

Ci vorrebbe un'invenzione
mappature astrali
tracce da inseguire
fili
polvere d'oro.

Un'invenzione ci vorrebbe
per capire
il fiato sospeso nel petto
dove posa ora il tuo sguardo
su quale stella coda cometa.

Oggi ho invocato la luce
pulito angoli
lucidato l'altrove
acceso fuoco e mirra
sperando sia questa la strada giusta
l'orizzonte e il verticale assieme.

6. Romero, *Salto mortale.*

If Only There Were an Invention

If only there were an invention
to shorten distances
the right path in the sky
the moon born with water.

If only there were an invention
astral mappings
traces to follow
threads
gold dust.

An invention is what we need
to understand
with bated breath
where you now direct your gaze
on which star tail comet.

Today I've invoked light
cleaned corners
polished the elsewhere
lit fire and myrrh
hoping this is the right way
at once horizon and vertical.

Chiedo perdono[7]

Chiedo perdono
chiedo perdono per essere guscio
chiedo perdono
chiedo perdono perché ostruisco l'uccello fragile del mio fervore.
Chiedo perdono per essere al passo con il tempo
il tempo degli assassini
delle amare amarezze
degli amarcord.
Chiedo perdono
e vorrei tornare al volo
al piumaggio sotto le orme del sole
a becchettare la terra in festa.

Da una vita che sono orba[8]

Da una vita che sono orba
stringo le palpebre e vedo solo immagini sbiadite.
Gli occhi s'incrociano e faccio paura agli altri.
Una pupilla fissa un continente abbandonato
l'altra si ostina a rimanere qui.
Per non parlare delle mani
scrivono lettere storte
non so nemmeno se sono mancina.
E la bocca; rigide labbra serrate
una lingua che balla persa tra i denti
sbagliando tutte le doppie
le è *aperte la* s *sonora e quella sorda.*
Le gambe vorrebbero alzarsi e andare via per strade lontane
ma nel tentativo inciampano e una s'attorciglia nell'altra.
Il corpo intero è un Pinocchio aggrovigliato

---

7. Romero, *Salto mortale.*

8. Romero, *Salto mortale.*

I Ask Forgiveness

I ask forgiveness
I ask forgiveness for being a shell
I ask forgiveness
I ask forgiveness for hampering the fragile bird of my fervor.
I ask forgiveness for being in line with the times
the time of killers
of bitter bitterness
of *amarcord*.
I ask forgiveness
and wish I could return to flying
to plumage under the sun's tracks
to pecking at the cheering earth.

All My Life I've Been Blind

All my life I've been blind
I squeeze my eyelids and see only faded images.
My eyes cross and I scare other people.
One pupil stares at a continent left behind
the other stubbornly remains here.
Not to mention my hands
that write crooked letters
I don't even know if I'm left handed.
And my mouth: stiff lips sealed tight
tongue dancing aimlessly around my teeth
missing all the double consonants
the open *è* the voiced and unvoiced *s*.
My legs would like to stand and walk away on distant roads
but in trying stumble and one twists around the other.
My entire body is a tangled up Pinocchio

fantoccio complesso per burattinai esperti
difficile trovare la sincronia tra i mondi annodati l'uno nell'altro
e mentre dalla platea urlano the show must go on!
ballo una pizzica stordita
aspettando la fata turchina
che mi doni pelle e ossa e un valzer morbido da ballare
o una chacarera
e che mi aiuti ad attraversare i campi dei miracoli
le pance di balene
senza perdermi
perché si possa finalmente rintanare a casa la sera
dove Geppetto aspetta con una zuppa calda per cena.

a complex marionette for expert puppeteers
hard to find synchrony between worlds knotted together
and as the audience shouts *the show must go on!*
I dance a dizzy *pizzica*[3]
waiting for the Blue Fairy
to gift me skin and bones and a soft waltz to dance
or a *chacarera*[4]
and to help me cross the fields of miracles
the bellies of whales
without getting lost
in order to finally hunker down at home in the evening
where Geppetto is waiting with warm soup for supper.

---

3. A genre of folk music and dance that originated in the Salento peninsula in Apulia, part of the larger family of the Southern Italian tarantella. The *pizzica* has a number of variations, most notably the *pizzica pizzica,* a couples dance, and the *pizzica tarantata,* a frenzied hypnotic dance used in the ancient healing ritual against the bite of the tarantula.

4. A genre of folk music and courtship dance that originated in the rural province of Santiago del Estero, in Argentina. It is danced in couples, with no contact between the partners except for a final embrace.

Barbara Serdakowski

L'attente[1]

Quand l'astre opaque s'enlisera au loin derrière les eaux
Quando l'astro opaco sprofonderà all'orizzonte dietro le acque

Il ne faudra plus attendre longtemps
Non ci sarà più tanto da aspettare

Il tempo fila ma non si spezza

Time has come now como nunca antes
Egli è giunto ora, come mai prima

Qui e adesso
Mi circonda indeciso

Puis il glisse et glisse à l'infini
Poi scivola, scivola via all'infinito

Demande-moi encore:
Chiedimelo ancora:

Pourquoi?… Pourquoi?… Pourquoi?…
Perché?… Perché?… Perché?…

Your voice so close arrastrandome como las mareas
La tua voce così vicina che mi rastrella come le maree

Dziś już nie mam siły aby jutro mieć

1. This selection of poems by Barbara Serdakowski appeared in *Sagarana* 7 (April 2002). They have also been included in a collection of Serdakowski's poems, *Così nuda* (Rome: Edizioni Ensemble, 2012). The versions included in this anthology were provided by the author.

L'Attente

Quand l'astre opaque s'enlisera au loin derrière les eaux
When the opaque star sinks behind the watery horizon

Il ne faudra plus attendre longtemps
There won't be much longer to wait

Time slips away but doesn't break

Time has come now como nunca antes
It has arrived now, as never before

Here and now
Hesitantly surrounding me

Puis il glisse et glisse à l'infini
Then drifting, drifting endlessly away

Demande-moi encore:
Ask me again:

Pourquoi?… Pourquoi?… Pourquoi?…
Why?… Why?… Why?…

Your voice so close arrastrandome como las mareas
Your voice so close raking me like the tides

Dziś już nie mam siły aby jutro mieć

Oggi non ho più la forza per averne domani

La force qui m'emporte au loin des voix, au loin des saisons
La forza che mi porta via lontano dalle voci, lontano dalle stagioni.

Chi non l'ha vista?… la luce?
Se guardi sulle tue pene non si riflette.
Per piacere ancora una volta

Pero no me mires con tus ojos sabios de mi
Ma non mi guardare con i tuoi occhi sapienti di me

As I stand here with you helpless, out of breath.
Mentre sto qui con te, impotente, senza fiato

Je sers dans mes poings les moignons de ma vie au-dessus de la mer
Sopra il mare stringo nei pugni i monconi della mia vita

Incrédule, je sème
Incredula, semino,

et peu à peu les vagues se figent…
e poco a poco i flutti si rapprendono…

Hoy se pararon las ondas del mar.
Oggi si sono fermate le onde del mare.

Today I have no strength left for tomorrow

La force qui m'emporte au loin des voix, au loin des saisons.
The strength that carries me away from the voices, away from the seasons.

Who didn't see it?… the light?
If you look on your sufferings it's not reflected.
One more time please

Pero no me mires con tus ojos sabios de mi
But don't look at me with your knowing eyes

As I stand here with you helpless, out of breath.

Je sers dans mes poings les moignons de ma vie au-dessus de la mer
Above the sea, my fists clench the stumps of my life

Incrédule, je sème
Incredulous, I sow,

et peu à peu les vagues se figent…
and little by little the swells congeal…

Hoy se pararon las ondas del mar.
Today the sea waves have come to a standstill.

Quando il giorno si alza triste

Quando il giorno si alza triste
Non saprei dirti cosa fare
Ma ci provo senza fine.

Et les mots, raisins, se fermentent
E le parole, uve, si fermentano

Nei silenzi lasciati di riserva per dopo.
Le raccolgo come posso

Mais la brume se lève déjà
Ma la nebbia già si alza

Upon my naked shame
Sulla mia nuda vergogna.

Ancora una volta il domani è venuto
Sempre costante all'improvviso.
Verrai anche tu?

Ce matin, ponctuel, ou plus tard, quand je ferais semblant déjà de ne plus t'attendre?
Stamattina puntuale, o più tardi, quando già faccio finta di non aspettarti più?

Le castagne bruciate nelle tasche con le pietre, il lichene e anche sempre quelle mie parole.

E mi dirai
Ti voglio, ti voglio, ti voglio bene
Forse basterà; com'è bastato tutte le altre volte,
Oggi dunque non potrà mai essere diverso.

When the Day Gets up Sad

When the day gets up sad
I couldn't tell you what to do
But I try over and over again.

Et les mots, raisins, se fermentent
And words, grapes, ferment

In silences set aside for later.
I harvest them any way I can

Mais la brume se lève déjà
But the fog is already lifting

Upon my naked shame

Once again tomorrow has come
Constant as always, all of a sudden.
Will you come too?

Ce matin, ponctuel, ou plus tard, quand je ferais semblant déjà
de ne plus t'attendre?
This morning, right on time, or later, when I'm already pretending
to be done waiting for you?

Burnt chestnuts in your pockets with rocks, lichen and also,
always, those words of mine.

And you'll tell me
I want you I want you I want to love you
Perhaps it'll be enough; as it was every other time,
So it can never be different today.

Guardo ancora più lontano, lontano non è poi così lontano,
Nel caleidoscopio vedo tanti tuoi giorni
Rossi, gialli, flessuosi, tutti, anche con le dita

Mille yeux écarquillés
Mille occhi esterrefatti

E ancora noi due davanti, insieme, lontani, davanti alla TV.

Mangia, mangia, fuori piove e dentro di noi
C'è il di fuori rinchiuso ancora per un po'.
Sfilano tutti quelli che conosco, uno, due, uno ad uno,
Sorridevano ancora l'altra volta ma oggi non mi guardano più
Allora alzo gli occhi su su su!

Fontaines, yeux fontaines
Fontane, occhi fontane,

Acque fredde, alte in cielo
Cipressi, monti e i miei seni ancorati alla bocca avida
del momento che passa, dello ieri, del domani.
Voglio, posso, esco, vado!

But you ask me: How? Again? More?
Ma tu mi chiedi: Come? Ancora? Di più?

Il giorno lo vedremo come sempre dal mattino
Leggerò l'avvenire dalle numerose nuvole
E poi metterò sugl'occhi tutte le mie due mani.

I look even farther away, faraway isn't so far after all,
In the kaleidoscope, I see so many of your days
Red, yellow, limber, all of them, with fingers too

Mille yeux écarquillés
One thousand astounded eyes

And still the two of us up front, together, distant, in front of the TV

Eat, eat, it's raining outside and inside of us
There is the outside, shut in for a little while longer.
Everyone I know passes by, one, two, one by one,
They were still smiling the other time but today they are no longer looking at me
So I look up up up!

Fontaines, yeux fontaines
Fountains, fountain eyes,

Cold waters, high up in the sky
Cypresses, hills and my breasts anchored to the greedy mouth of the passing moment, of yesterday, of tomorrow.
I want, I can, I go out, I leave!

But you ask me: How? Again? More?

The morning as always will tell us how the day will turn out
I'll read the future in the numerous clouds
Then I'll place both my hands on my eyes.

Langues et raisons

Penser en langues
Pensare in lingue

Qui s'entremêlent toutes semblables et roses
Che s'intrecciano tutte simili e rosa

My hands are open
Le mie mani sono aperte

devant la porte fermée
davanti alla porta chiusa

et les enfants s'accrochent aux barreaux des fenêtres
e i bambini si aggrappano alle sbarre delle finestre

Look at me
guardami

Regarde
Guarda

Don't you see I can't hear you?
Non vedi che non ti posso sentire?

Se non fai lo sforzo non potrai.

Je rêve en concepts
Sogno in concetti

En unités ou en bites
In unità o in bites

Mes pensées en ASCII voyagent
I miei pensieri viaggiano in ASCII

Langues et raisons

Penser en langues
Thinking in tongues

Qui s'entremêlent toutes semblables et roses
That get entwined, all alike and pink

My hands are open

devant la porte fermée
in front of the closed door

et les enfants s'accrochent aux barreaux des fenêtres
and the children cling on to the window bars

Look at me

Regarde
Look

Don't you see I can't hear you?

If you don't make the effort you won't be able to.

Je rêve en concepts
I dream in concepts

En unités ou en bites
In units or in bytes

Mes pensées en ASCII voyagent
My thoughts travel in ASCII

transportées par une onde invisible réchauffée
trasportate da un'onda invisibile riscaldata

Can you fax me a little time?
Mi mandi un po' di tempo per fax?

Demain ne sera plus pareil
Domani non sarà più lo stesso

Ani jutro, ani nigdy
Né domani né mai

Car le droit de veto, vote, tove, tevo, evot…
Perché il diritto di veto, di voto, tove, tevo, evot…

will divide in half what was already given away.
dividerà in due quello che è stato già dato via.

Et pourtant tu disais…
Eppure dicevi

Encore et encore
Ancora ed ancora

Believe in, believe me,
Credi, credimi,

Non credo più, basta eppure…

Les années changent notre monde
Gli anni cambiano il nostro mondo

without us realizing
senza che noi ce ne accorgiamo

et seuls nos reflets dans la glace
e solo i nostri riflessi nello specchio

transportées par une onde invisible réchauffée
carried by an invisible heated wave

Can you fax me a little time?

Demain ne sera plus pareil
Tomorrow will never be the same

Ani jutro, ani nigdy
Neither tomorrow, nor ever

Car le droit de veto, vote, tove, tevo, evot…
Because the right to veto, to vote, tove, tevo, evot…

will divide in half what was already given away.

Et pourtant tu disais…
And yet you used to say

Encore et encore
Again and again

Believe in, believe me,

I no longer believe, that's enough and yet…

Les années changent notre monde
The years change our world

without us realizing

et seuls nos reflets dans la glace
and only our reflections in the mirror

nous rappellent
ci ricordano

com'era dolce per noi
how sweet for us was

il nostro tempo di allora
our time back then

and how much part of us
e come parte di noi

does not belong anymore.
non appartiene più.

Nasze życie bez celu
La nostra vita senza meta

is spinning and calling
gira e chiama

le mate call of du caribou
il richiamo del caribou

ou le canard decoy?
o dello zimbello

La luce si fa

mais pas pour longtemps
ma non per molto

car déjà les lumières éblouissantes s'éteignent
perché già le luci accecanti si spengono

et l'obscurité de l'avenir surprend par son intolérance.
e l'oscurità del futuro sorprende per la sua intolleranza.

nous rappellent
remind us

com'era dolce per noi
how sweet for us was

il nostro tempo di allora
our time back then

and how much part of us

does not belong anymore.

Nasze życie bez celu
Our aimless life

is spinning and calling

le mate call of du caribou
the mating call of the caribou

ou le canard decoy?
or the decoy duck?

Light is shed

mais pas pour longtemps
but not for long

car déjà les lumières éblouissantes s'éteignent
because the blinding lights are already going out

et l'obscurité de l'avenir surprend par son intolérance.
and the obscurity of the future is shockingly intolerant.

A present without past
Un presente senza passato

a past without present.
un passato senza presente.

Ma il domani esisterà ancora
quando verrà il suo tempo?
Per quanto tempo?

L'espoir,
La speranza

Tel une fuite de gaz
come una fuga di gas

nous endort innocents
ci addormenta innocenti

sans savoir que c'est pour le long voyage.
senza sapere che è per il lungo viaggio.

Le fait de le dire
Il fatto di dirlo

avec les mots, les silences
con le parole, i silenzi

L'incommunication volontaire
L'incomunicazione volontaria

that creeps in unaware
che s'incunea inconsapevole

con tutte le sue radici

et les mille semences.
e i mille semi.

A present without past

a past without present.

But will tomorrow still exist
when its time comes?
For how long?

L'espoir,
Hope,

Tel une fuite de gaz
Like a gas leak

nous endort innocents
lulls us to sleep, clueless

sans savoir que c'est pour le long voyage.
unaware that it's for the long journey.

Le fait de le dire
Just saying it

avec les mots, les silences
with words, silences

L'incommunication volontaire
Voluntary noncommunication

that creeps in unaware

with all its roots

et les mille semences.
and a thousand seeds.

Mañana,

si le mañana vient,
se il mañana viene

avec ses aubes de délivrance,
con le sue albe liberatorie,

alors quizás, podremos estar juntos
allora forse, potremmo stare insieme

Po jakiemu?
Come?

En quelles langues?
In quali lingue?

En quelles raisons?
In quali ragioni?

Mañana,

si le mañana vient,
if mañana comes

avec ses aubes de délivrance,
with its liberating dawns,

alors quizás, podremos estar juntos
then perhaps, we'll be able to be together

Po jakiemu?
How?

En quelles langues?
In what tongues?

En quelles raisons?
In what reasons?

Terre

Una nave che parte

That carries my pirate spirit away from my roots
Che porta il mio spirito pirata lontano dalle radici

Yes I am the one that was once born there
Sì, sono quella che è nata là una volta

And my land is still that land
E la mia terra è sempre quella terra

Ma io non sono più io.
In prua, immortalata
Sono vento, legnificata, nuda, con la bandiera unicolore dei miei capelli
E fendo le acque, e sfido le torbide onde

Les tempêtes explosent sur mes traits de bois
Le tempeste scoppiano sui miei tratti di legno

Et mes seins nus s'offrent aux griffes des flots
E i miei seni nudi si offrono alle grinfie dei flutti

Décharnée, j'aboutis sur les sables des plages pérégrines
Scarnita, mi riverso sulle sabbie delle spiagge pellegrine

J'éventre, irrévérente les ports
Sventro, irriverente i porti

A jamás extraña a las huellas de las sirenas de mi tierra.
Per sempre estranea alle orme delle sirene della mia terra.

Lands

A ship that leaves

That carries my pirate spirit away from my roots

Yes I am the one that was once born there

And my land is still that land

But I'm no longer myself.
On the bow, immortalized
I'm wind, lignified, naked, with the single-color flag of
my hair
And I plough through the waters, and challenge the turbid waves

Les tempêtes explosent sur mes traits de bois
Storms blast on my wooden features

Et mes seins nus s'offrent aux griffes des flots
And my bare breasts surrender to the billows' clutches

Décharnée, j'aboutis sur les sables des plages pérégrines
Stripped to the bone, I end up on the sands of peregrine shores

J'éventre, irrévérente les ports
Irreverent, I eviscerate the harbors

A jamás extraña a las huellas de las sirenas de mi tierra.
Forever alien to the footprints of my land's sirens.

Jeszcze raz

I suoni delle parole sono ormai stanchi
E non hanno più neanche il significato.

Jeszcze raz
Ancora una volta

Tu avais raison et moi tort
Avevi ragione ed io torto

Avoir raison jusqu'à n'en avoir plus de raisons
Avere ragione fino a non avere più ragioni

Rien, encore, hier et puis demain
Niente, ancora, ieri e poi domani

Vraiment sans plus savoir si ce que l'on fait reste ou devient
Senza veramente più sapere se quello che facciamo rimane
o diventa

Aussi inutile que la feuille qui pourrit dans l'eau
Così inutile come la foglia che marcisce nell'acqua

Too much or not enough
Troppo o troppo poco

Le jour naît toujours avec le même espoir
Il giorno nasce sempre con la stessa speranza

Et puis plus du tout
E poi nient'altro

Si tu supieras cuanto poco se de ti
Se sapessi quando poco so di te

Cuanto poco entiendo tus obras de hoy
Quanto poco capisco delle tue opere d'oggi

Jeszcze raz

Words sound tired now
And they've even lost their meaning.

Jeszcze raz
Once again

Tu avais raison et moi tort
You were right and I was wrong

Avoir raison jusqu'à n'en avoir plus de raisons
Being right to the point of having no reasons left to be right

Rien, encore, hier et puis demain
Nothing, again, yesterday and then tomorrow

Vraiment sans plus savoir si ce que l'on fait reste ou devient
No longer truly knowing if what we do endures
or becomes

Aussi inutile que la feuille qui pourrit dans l'eau
As useless as a leaf rotting in water

Too much or not enough

Le jour naît toujours avec le même espoir
The day always dawns with the same hope

Et puis plus du tout
And then nothing else

Si tu supieras cuanto poco se de ti
If you knew how little I know about you

Cuanto poco entiendo tus obras de hoy
How little I understand your current deeds

Cuanto me sorprenden tus palabras
Quanto mi sorprendono le tue parole

Y tus inconstancias
E le tue incostanze

E le parti che ormai interpretiamo
Senza neanche fermarci un istante per recitare meglio

Where were you yesterday when I wanted to speak to you?
Dov'eri, ieri quando volevo parlare con te?

Where was the breeze when the sun was too hot?
Dov'era la brezza quando il sole era troppo caldo?

And where were my words of comfort?
E dov'erano le mie parole di conforto?

And my riding sabre, and my riot shield
E la mia sciabola da battaglia e il mio scudo da sommossa

My sunglasses and all the clothes I wear to be again something
I want others to believe.
I miei occhiali da sole e tutti quei vestiti che porto per essere ancora
una volta qualcosa che voglio che gli altri credano.

Reste près de moi
Rimani vicino a me

Je veux encore sentir comme les jours nous ont séparés
Voglio sentire come i giorni ci hanno separato

Pouvoir sentir encore la rage des instants qui se perdent devant moi
Poter sentire ancora la rabbia degli istanti che si perdono davanti a me

Des choses qui s'accumulent
Delle cose che si accumulano

Cuanto me sorprenden tus palabras
How surprised I am by your words

Y tus inconstancias
By your inconsistencies

And the roles we now play
Without pausing even an instant to improve our performance

Where were you yesterday when I wanted to speak to you?

Where was the breeze when the sun was too hot?

And where were my words of comfort?

And my riding sabre, and my riot shield

My sunglasses and all the clothes I wear to be again something
I want others to believe.

Reste près de moi
Stay close to me

Je veux encore sentir comme les jours nous ont séparés
I want to feel how the days have driven us apart

Pouvoir sentir encore la rage des instants qui se perdent devant moi
To be able to feel rage again for the moments being lost before me

Des choses qui s'accumulent
For the things piling up

Des joies que je n'arrive plus à accrocher.
Delle gioie che non riesco più a catturare.

Veo mis palabras que no te llegan más y me quedo con ellas
Vedo le mie parole che non ti raggiungono più e rimango con esse

Como los pedazos rotos de la muñeca de porcelana.
Come i pezzi rotti della bambola di porcellana.

Trying to see in every single piece the whole.
Provando a scorgere in ognuno dei singoli pezzi, il tutto.

Des joies que je n'arrive plus à accrocher.
For the joys I can't catch any longer.

Veo mis palabras que no te llegan más y me quedo con ellas
I see my words no longer reaching you and I remain behind with them.

Como los pedazos rotos de la muñeca de porcelana.
Like the broken pieces of a porcelain doll

Trying to see in every single piece the whole.

♒

Laila Wadia

Kalì Red[1]

After seven years spent polishing the West, I'm becoming convinced that the law of equality trumps the law of difference. This thesis of mine is the result of an olfactory observation: over time, shoes stink. Ms. Anna's shoes smell — she works in a bank and wraps them in lavender scented bags. So do Ms. Matilda's — I iron for her every other Thursday. And no exception for the designer boots of Ms. Delia, who keeps them in a precious walnut shoe cabinet in the hallway lined with Carrara marble. It doesn't matter how much you spend. Aided and abetted by weather and the passage of time, shoes end up smelling like the carrion from which they were torn.

I've been asking myself why for a long time and have finally reached the following conclusion. The ladies who pay me to keep their apartments clean surely don't hang around people who are less well off, and if they run across poverty on the street, they don't look it straight in the eye, so their consciences are clear. Their shoes, instead, have no escape. They're forced to mix with the rabble, to come into contact with madness and pain. Day after day, over common ground, they're infected with the trampled dignity of too many people. But this hasn't happened to one particular pair of shoes. Despite its knowledge of suffering, it has maintained its immaculate perfection. They were devil red patent leather with chili pepper heels. I was obsessed with them.

I'm a poor woman, but an honest one. I've never taken even a tissue without asking for permission first. But for those shoes, I confess that I would have made an exception. Luckily I managed

1. Laila Wadia, "Rosso Kalì," in *Se tutte le donne* (Siena: Barbera, 2012).

to kidnap them once in a while and return them before their owner noticed they were missing. When I knew that Mrs. Brambilla was going to spend the weekend at her beach house or her apartment in Cortina, I'd take them home with me. And then, in the studio apartment I shared with a roommate in a shabby San Siro building, the simple footwear became the avatar of the goddess Kalì. My roommate has never been able to understand my pathological fascination with an old pair of red shoes, the left one slightly stretched out to accommodate Mrs. Brambilla's bunion.

Nina and I share the same apartment, but live in different ways. My friend's corner is an emporium of hopes. Nina is an identity kleptomaniac. She was born in Bhopal in Northern India, the city sadly known for the Union Carbide accident. In 1984, a cloud of toxic gas escaped from the American-owned pesticide plant, causing thousands of deaths and hundreds of thousands of other injuries. I've heard that something similar happened in Seveso. But unlike the incident in Italy, in Bhopal they're still waiting for justice twenty-five years after the disaster, and Nina, like so many others, was forced to emigrate. She had to give up her aspirations, forget the person she could have been if the company's top executives had paid the slightest amount of attention to safety. Now, instead of the happy wife and contented mother she dreamed of becoming, she's only a servant. Still, as soon as she collects her paycheck, she rushes to buy a crystal vase, a wool jacket, or a lace doily. Owning the same things that rich people do gives her the illusion that she hasn't given up on her dreams, not even at the age of fifty-four. Her purchases are mere imitations of the originals, but thanks to Bangladeshi and Chinese stores, our apartment has become a showcase for low-cost dreams.

My corner, on the other hand, is white and stark. White bedspread. White wardrobe. White chair. White nightstand. White lamp. For Indians, white is the color of mourning, the hue of nirvana, of the absence of desire. But on some rare weekends, all of that Himalayan whiteness is desecrated by spicy hot red. Red is my obsession. White and black are clear-cut colors: they swallow your mind or free your soul, depending on your native culture. Red is promiscuous. Blood and passion. Paradise and purgatory. Ambivalent like the goddess Kalì. Red is vice — a woman's mouth chewing fresh tobacco leaves — but most of all red is happiness. A bride's sari. The *sindhoor* powder a married woman applies in the part of her hair. Red is the *tikka,* the vermillion dot she applies to her forehead every morning before leaving the house. Red the glass bangles she'll wear until her husband's death.

♒

As is the case with all the women I work for, I hardly ever see Mrs. Brambilla, and I wonder whether the difference between West and East can be summed up by the status of women. It seems to me that here in Milan, women must get out of the house in order to make it, whereas in India, to make it, they're frequently forced to remain buried at home. In any case, what's clear is that, in much of the world, women's free will is all too often still a pipe dream.

Even though the law firm she runs with her husband is located barely two blocks from their home, Mrs. Brambilla and I communicate through notes. Before completing an Italian evening course at the IAL,[2] I used to carry around a heavy Italian-Hindi dictionary to try to decipher her instructions.

Occasionally she comes home for lunch with her husband, but whereas the Ganges and its flooding tributaries flow out of her mouth — praise for my improved cooking skills thanks to the TV shows I watch while ironing, pleas to use less chili pepper, and astonishment at some unusual dish like bananas in ginger sauce — as soon as he sits at the table, the trickle that's in him runs completely dry, and Mr. Brambilla turns into one of the ceramic knick-knacks lying around the house. I never get more than a few grunts out of him.

2. IAL (Innovazione Apprendimento Lavoro) is a national network of workforce development agencies.

≈

Nina has tons of fun trying on the fur coats and accessories of the ladies she works for. I, instead, have zero interest in clothes. In the wintertime, I always wear a turtleneck and a pair of black pants. The only change in the summertime is the fabric. My ear and nose piercings have now closed up. In order to pay for my plane ticket, I was forced to sell both the large gold earrings I had been wearing since I was a child and my diamond nose stud.

When she came to Italy fifteen years ago, Nina brought saris from India. Not me. The sari, for me, is the outer layer of the woman's chrysalis — a protective shell that saved the goddess Sita when the monster Ravana threatened her honor. But it can also become a five-yard long fuse. Like many other women during that crazy summer in my native state of Gujarat in Northern India, I was forced to become a butterfly, to learn to fly prematurely, to rely only on my own wings. To flap them very hard in order to put out the fire of hatred between Hindus and Muslims. My red Sari, the one my mother had embroidered for my wedding, which was supposed to be celebrated six months later, was left behind to burn like everything else, red on red, an eye for an eye, blinding my village forever.

Nina doesn't believe that I've never tried to wear any of Mrs. Brambilla's clothes, not even the red shoes, not even for fun. But I can guarantee that I've never done it. Playing like a little girl with mom's shoes isn't one of my fancies for the simple reason that it's not part of my cultural baggage. First of all, my mother has never owned a pair of shoes. She had two pairs of slippers — one leather, the other plastic for rainy days. Back home, where people love to feel mother earth breathing under their feet, shoes are only for snobs. Heels are for rich, spoiled women. And red ones, in the collective imagination of my village, are only for whores. Furthermore, there is the belief that wearing somebody else's shoes means taking over their destiny.

Where I'm from, when they want to pretend to be grown-ups, little girls play with glass bracelets. But my mother's — two dozen thin bangles of scarlet glass dotted with gold, my passion when I was a child — exploded one by one, just as my dreams did.

⁂

"How is it possible that you never buy anything?" asks Nina, while trying to invade my space, free of consumerist trappings, with trinkets, her latest purchase at the St. Ambrogio feast. How can I make her understand that the more you have, the more it hurts when somebody rips it away from you? Glass bracelets, plastic sandals, leather sandals, mom, my sister, my father. My wedding sari. All ripped away. Everything. By red fire. I should hate red. And in fact I do. Fire red. Fear red. Red flags flying, covered in blood, in the name of a different god. The color of the end of my first life.

Fortunately, I was able to get away before going completely crazy. In Italy, ironically, many consider me lucky because, as a refugee, I had an easier time than others getting a residence permit. I think there are at least three words that should be banned in all languages because they are too subjective, too politicized, and hence a source of immense pain: luck, happiness, God.

I remember the greeting from the lawyer who helped with my regularization case: "Be happy, dear Prema," he told me.

I gave him a stunned look. Happy? What is happiness? Then, in the desperate search for a definition, I latched onto a color. Red. My enemy. Strange thing, the human mind, when it's given free rein. It makes illogical turns. After my life in India burned down, I willed myself to hate red. In place of the heart prone to bleeding, I transplanted a freezer. But it's silly to think that freezing is the same as forgetting. Moving to another country is a palliative. Adopting a different language is a farce. Making more money is an illusion. Sadness is not driven out by higher purchasing power, and loneliness has no permanent residence.

Stateless, they wander in constant search of new victims. But red is also Kalì, destroyer of evil, goddess of women. Mother Kalì. Red is my atavistic happiness.

♒

Mrs. Brambilla loved them too. I could tell by the way she took them off when she came home. She didn't push one foot against the other, as she did with ordinary shoes, quickly ruining their inner edges. She cared for her red shoes as she would have cared for the children she was never able to have. She wrapped them in a soft cloth and stored them in a box, in the shoe cabinet off the bathroom.

As I've already mentioned, I don't know the people I work for. After a brief interview and the handing over of the keys, they communicate primarily in writing: Prema, clean the bathroom today. Prema, can you do the windows? Prema, here's the list for the supermarket.

Like a detective, I've gotten to know them through their homes. Ms. Anna's house is modern, with a living room full of the strangest paintings. One, for instance, is a two by two meter canvas full of black dots with a red one in the center.

"That is our investment for our old age, so please remember to be very careful not to spray anything on it," she warned me the first time we met.

Sometimes I stare at that painting, trying to make sense of it. I see this country more from the inside than from the outside, from the bellies of homes more than from the streets. I try to understand its innards and not let myself be deceived by outward appearances. For me, that painting represents the dream of every Italian: to be the red dot in a sea of black dots.

Ms. Matilda's home looks like a thrift shop. It's a challenge to clean because there's old stuff everywhere, old vases, old dishes, old glasses, old embroidered handbags. Maybe her fascination with the antique is a sign of her discomfort in the present?

Ms. Delia's villa is perhaps the most solid and classic house, passed down from generation to generation. I think it's really nice to sleep in a bed where your grandparents loved each other, and you were still a random note in the incomplete symphony of their destiny. Ms. Dalia has a passion for pearls. She has lots of them — necklaces, bracelets, brooches — scattered around the house. Pearls remind me of human frailty and the hope that all believers share. With the rosary, Catholics pray to the Virgin Mary. By using the *jap mala*, Hindus invoke Shiva's benevolence. And Muslim prayer beads bring human supplications closer to Allah's ear. Words, in the mouth of a true believer, are always pearls, never stones.

Mrs. Brambilla's home, instead, is divided into zones. Her romantic tastes are at odds with her husband's technological ones. The only promiscuous zone is the kitchen, where a digital clock tolerates the embrace of a rag doll and clay pots nestle in the womb of the microwave oven. As for the rest, they each have their own study, their own sitting room, even their own bedroom. At first, I thought the room with the plasma TV and the headboard with built-in stereo system was the guest room, since I hadn't needed to make the bed in six years.

An observant woman like me should have noticed the changes with no need for an official announcement. The first time Mrs. Brambilla forgot to leave my pay, for instance. It wasn't like her. She was always precise and punctual. I felt awkward having to call her at work, and fortunately, they put me through to her husband, who came immediately to bring me my monthly wages and apologies.

When she stayed home one morning, I asked her if there was something the matter. She was putting her collection of dolls in a big box and didn't answer when I asked if she wanted a hand.

"Leave me alone, please. There's nothing, don't you see?" she replied in a flat voice.

"What do you mean, there's nothing," I screamed to myself, confusing my poor knowledge of the Italian language with my rich knowledge of loss. "You have everything! A house full of possessions, a job full of rewards, a considerate husband. Saying you have nothing means living with a dark heart." Pain makes us self-centered, and mine, dormant but not eradicated, made me insensitive to the fact that darkness was precisely the disease slowly taking hold of Mrs. Brambilla. Unfortunately, we tend to judge others by our own experiences, but pain and happiness are entities that can't be compared. They can only be added to, accumulated, woman after woman, person after person, in the infinite red of the universe.

The following week, I found her at home on the three days I spend cleaning her house from nine to two, and then Mr. Brambilla asked me to please come every day to keep an eye on her and keep her company so she didn't spend too much time alone.

She didn't look sick to me, just deeply sad. She tried to read but couldn't focus. I checked out the title of the novel she was trying to finish. It was *Follow Your Heart.* My first instinct was to tell her to forget about a novel with such a subversive title. Following your own heart is a gift that angels seldom grant.

I spoke to Nina about wanting to tell Mrs. Brambilla that two women like us, so close now that we were syncing our periods, should learn to sync our hearts. With a cynical smile, Nina replied that an Italian woman — and what's more, a lawyer — would never confide in an Indian housekeeper. Thinking otherwise, she said, made me presumptuous. "Why not?" I insisted. She, blond like an ear of wheat that instead of stronger becomes more fragile with maturity; me, coarse *bajra* flour, ground by destiny again and again, to the point of losing my desires — why couldn't we mix, join forces to form a sincere friendship?

Mrs. Brambilla repaid my compassion with irritation, picking on me for every little thing: "Why did you move the picture frame with dad's photo? Who told you to put away the book I'm reading? Where are my glasses, I'm sure you moved them while you were dusting!" It was becoming harder and harder to serve her. I had known despair, and I was very familiar with economic degradation, with desolation, but I had never come across depression. Single-mindedly obsessed with the yin and yang of red, I had to learn that there is a worse color. A terrible color, without emotions, without hope, without life. Gray. And depression is nothing but a never-ending cold sheet soaked in ashes.

Shortly thereafter, she stopped talking. She no longer directed a greeting or even a reproach at me. And the cloak of silence that at first was her nest, became her grave. I would have liked to shake her. Ma'am, why don't you go to work any more? Why don't you talk, cry, scream? At times, handing her a cup of coffee or tea, I held her icy hands for a moment in an attempt to infuse her with my thoughts, to provoke a reaction. Instead nothing. And what I deluded myself into thinking was complicit silence was nothing more than empty silence.

Once, on the street, I saw the remains of a pigeon that had been devoured by some animal. Only the wings and the rib cage were left. That could have been me, I thought. They tried to devour me. But I held on tight to my wings, and they could only pluck my feathers, not strip my flesh. When the enemy is external you can fight it, you can try to defend yourself, or you can flee. But when the enemy is within you, there is sadly no escape.

Every time we passed by a Chinese store, Nina pushed me to buy a pair of shoes like Mrs. Brambilla's. If I was too much of a snob for shoes made in China, I could even afford a pair made in Italy. Nina scolded me all the time for my thrift. "Look, Red Valentino. Who are you saving for anyway?" At the sight of my glistening eyes, Nina apologized. She said that her mouth was bigger than her brain. That she was rude and inconsiderate. Her aggressiveness was because of her forced separation from home, the endless lies of her double life. In her home country, nobody knew that she worked as a cleaning lady. They thought she was a secretary in a big company. They wouldn't have understood how an accountant who graduated at the top of her class — the apple of her parents' eyes, fruit of immense sacrifices to allow her to study — didn't have a prestigious job.

≈

Mrs. Brambilla left the house twice a week to go to the doctor. Sometimes she came back smiling, but most of the time she holed up in her bedroom, saying she wasn't hungry. Forced to eat alone, her husband began to garnish his grunts with a few sad smiles.

"I'm not worthy of being a woman," she whispered one morning, sitting on the couch by the window. "I don't even know how to clean house. Look how you are dusting even the baseboard. I would never have thought of that. Perhaps that's why I can't become a mother."

It was the first time she shared such a confidence with me.

"We can talk if you want," I said to her as I crouched to sit on the floor. "I am like a sister."

Mrs. Brambilla gave a jolt. "Sister!" It was a muffled scream. "You are not my sister. You are an object. Something my husband bought for me. He thinks that with money you can buy everything. Now he's telling me to buy a baby. Maybe go to India and rent the uterus of some wretch. I'm sterile, you know. I'm sterile here, here, and here" — she pointed at her sex, her heart, and her head. "My country is sterile. It doesn't generate anything anymore, except for hate. We hate you all, you foreigners with over-fertile wombs, but we need you, and so we hate you even more because nothing makes a human being weaker than being dependent on others."

I stared at her as, ever more agitated, she kept on uttering words that made no sense to me. "Bring me my shoes," she ordered. "Now! I said right now!"

My heart, which was softening from her pain, hardened at once. I handed them to her, frostily.

"Put them on me!" she shouted.

You can be suffocated by your sorrows, I thought, noticing that her feet were so swollen they didn't fit in her shoes.

"Not these, you idiot! I didn't tell you to bring me these! Don't you know that the time for red shoes is over?"

"Why am I even bothering," I thought, looking for her black ankle boots. But then I remembered her husband's words: "My wife is gravely ill, Prema. She needs you. Please don't abandon us." He — that man of so few words — said it with such sincerity that I would have liked to hug him. And those very words, dictated perhaps only by necessity, sprayed my white, arctic world with red.

I had to learn a lot, and very quickly, about depression, an illness that people in my country, more inclined to walk arm in arm with its stepmother, despair, don't seem to understand.

Mrs. Brambilla, under the influence of powerful psychotropic drugs, didn't remember the terrible words she said to me or her husband. But those ugly words weren't red with anger. They were black, reflecting the decomposing of her true lifeblood. In her mind, memories of her previous life, her identity, her feelings, were rotting away. Only very rarely did she let a ray of sunlight penetrate the tunnel into which she had slipped.

"Thanks," she told me once, holding my hands. "Thank you for supporting me. The others have all disappeared — those who called themselves friends, sister, mother. There's no one left but you, the one all the others call a foreigner."

♒

It was eleven on a Tuesday night when Mr. Brambilla called me on the phone. "Mimosa, my wife, Mrs. Brambilla, did she tell you she'd be coming home late?" he asked.

I said no, but when I heard that she wasn't back yet, I rushed to their house. "She went out in her red shoes," I noted, hovering between hope and despair. "Then she's at the doctor's."

Mr. Brambilla shook his head. "I also thought that she might still be at Bembo's, but he says that she left around six. Now I'm beginning to worry because she hasn't answered her cell phone for more than six hours. But right now I'm going to drive you home. It's dangerous to take public transport at this hour. You shouldn't have even come this late. What if something happened to you? So where exactly do you live? Do you realize you've been working for us for seven years, and I don't even know where you live? I know nothing about you, not a thing. Are you happy with us? We appreciate your work very much, you know. Mimma, Mimosa, says all the time that she wouldn't know how to get by without you."

I couldn't hold back the tears. It was the weeping of someone who hadn't been shown kindness for too long, but Mr. Brambilla mistook it for concern for his wife.

"You really care about her, don't you?" he said, touched. "And to think that at first I put up such a fight about letting you into our home. I'm a real jerk. But with all the daily scaremongering in the press, you let yourself be infected without even asking why."

I nodded to say that it didn't matter. He certainly wasn't responsible for depriving me of my dignity. My own people had seen to that. Those who have experienced the flames of intolerance, borne the unbearable, looked the devil in the face and realized he looks like them, surely won't be scared by the words of some fool who feels superior only for having a lighter complexion.

Coming out of the building, we ran into two Carabinieri, and one of them was holding a plastic bag containing a pair of red shoes with chili pepper heels.

"We've found a pair of shoes, they're…"

"The hibiscus red of the mimosa. Paradise red, purgatory red," I finished the sentence to myself.

In subdued tones, the men in uniform informed us that the woman who was wearing them — or rather, who had taken them off before carrying out her desperate act — no longer needed them where she was now. Two liquid diamonds streamed down the ashen face of Mr. Brambilla as he began to shake badly.

The policemen invited him to follow them to the hospital to identify the body. Turning towards me, Mr. Brambilla asked me to please stay at his house that night. He added that he would compensate me for my trouble. He couldn't bear the thought of coming back to an empty house.

"Of course," I said, feeling shame for having accused Mrs. Brambilla of ingratitude, of weakness, while I was the truly ungrateful one. I, who had been burned in the bonfire of ethnic hatred, but was reluctant to believe that scars can heal. Poor Mrs. Brambilla, instead, was slowly consumed by an inner pyre that no one was able to extinguish. She had to take care of it herself, at night, choosing the twelfth floor of a skyscraper as the way to escape her unbearable pain.

I went back inside and took a close look at her home once full of rag dolls. Then I looked inside my mind filled with memories, resentments, and regrets. Exactly the same. I slowly understood that Mrs. Brambilla and I were both opposites and identical, and together, in a dimension that knows no race, no time, and no space, we moved into Kalì's home.

"You can have them, if you want," said her husband, offering them to me. His eyes indicated that he was aware of the occasional kidnappings that the red shoes were subjected to. "I think it was her way of saying that she didn't throw away happiness, only her body that was no longer happy. She used to say that red is the color of joy."

≈

There is an old Indian superstition about wearing somebody else's shoes, but I no longer believe in superstitions. We each have our destiny, and we are just fellow travelers on a long and often steep road. Nevertheless, on that stretch we travel along together, if you never step into another's shoes it's like spending your entire life in a gray armchair staring into the void. If you just look at them, on impulse you would say that, for me, these shoes are large. But what to the eye, often cynical and superficial, appears to be just an empty space, to the prudent and farsighted heart becomes a wish for happiness.

≈

FRIENDS FOR LIFE[3]

CHARACTERS

SHANTI, a young Indian woman

LULE, a young Albanian woman, who is always elegantly dressed

MARINKA, a young Bosnian woman, tomboy. Her appearance is always shabby. She has problems with pronunciation and occasionally uses Triestine dialect.

ROSE BUD, a young Chinese woman, who frequently makes pronunciation mistakes and misuses idiomatic expressions

KAMLA, a young Indian girl

LAURA, a middle-aged Italian teacher. She always wears an EMERGENCY[4] sweatshirt.

MR. ROSSO, an old Italian man

---

3. This is the translation of the short version of *Amiche per la pelle,* a play written by Wadia as a contribution to a festival that took place in Trieste in 2009 (organized by the cultural association Spaesati). It was conceived as a "social project, to give visibility to non-professional actors, and to involve the community" (personal email, March 19, 2018). The play (unpublished) is based on the homonymous novel (Edizioni E/O, 2007), which was adapted for the screen as *Babylon Sisters* (2017). In a Skype conversation with students at the University of Iowa, Wadia stated that she had had in mind a different title for the novel ("Via Ungaretti" or "Lezioni d'italiano"), and that the publisher chose the title *Amiche per la pelle.* The publisher may have had in mind a pun, alluding to the chromatic difference of some immigrants, but Wadia was fine with the title because she is intrigued by the Italian idiom "amiche per la pelle," which means "I would give my life for you" (*pelle,* skin, in Italy is a metonymy for *vita,* life). Instead of calling attention to the differences that may divide us (skin color), the idiom calls attention to what brings us close: the force that inspires solidarity, caring for another to the point of sacrificing one's own life.

4. EMERGENCY is an Italian NGO founded in 1994 to provide free and high-quality medical and surgical care to victims of wars, anti-personnel mines, and poverty.

SHANTI'S HOUSE

THE LANDLORD'S FUNERAL AND THE PHONE CALL TO FIND AN ITALIAN TEACHER

NARRATOR'S VOICE: Trieste's historic center has three types of housing. There's the elegant Borgo Teresiano, commissioned by Austria's Empress Maria Teresa. There's the populous old town, with its tight-knit apartment buildings, which has recently been christened Zona Urban and now features charming hotels and eclectic lofts. Via Ungaretti, however, belongs to a third zone, the one that seems to be often forgotten by both nature and City Hall. Our story takes place at building number 25, which today finds itself immersed in a dream-like atmosphere.

LULE: Where are you going dressed like that?

MARINKA: You look beautiful! You need to vear[5] Indian clothes more often.

LULE: Are you crazy? She can't be wearing white at a funeral.

BUD: Why not?

SHANTI: Our home we use white for dead.

LULE: Good grief, you've been in Italy for eight years, don't you know that here people wear black at a funeral?

---

5. Errors in pronunciation, grammar and idiomatic expressions have been rendered by directly translating the error whenever Italian and English usage coincides (as in some instances of omitted/misused article and incorrect agreement of subject and verb), or by transposing the mistake to reproduce the foreign accent. In the sentence above, for instance, where the mistake is conveyed through phonetic spelling, the wrong pronunciation of "qu" as "kv" ("*Kv*anto sei bella! Devi mettere abiti indiani più spesso") has been transposed by replacing "w" with "v" in a different word: "You look beautiful! You need to *v*ear Indian clothes more often."

BUD: We are foreigners. We have different traditions and consumptions.

LULE: Customs. Traditions and customs.

MARINKA: But also different consumptions! At least, most of us.

SHANTI: Shall I go change?

MARINKA: No no, don't give her the satisfaction. Plus the dead don't give a damn how we dress.

LULE: *(pointing at Marinka's outfit)* But the living do!

BUD: To integrate it's more important to take lessons. Did you bring the telephone number, Lule?

LULE: Shall I call her? *(The others nod.)* Hello, Ms. Laura? Good morning, my name is Lule Dardini. I read your advertisement in the local *Mercatino*. We're a group of friends who would like some Italian lessons.... Yes, thank you, you're very kind, I know I speak well. I'd still come to improve my lexicon and be in good company. *(Marinka rolls her eyes.)* We were thinking once a week. We are neighbors. *(Shanti makes a gesture that the classes can be held at her house.)*

BUD: Wednesday afternoon is better. Restaurant is closed.

LULE: Did you hear that? She's my Chinese neighbor. She's got problems especially with the pronunciation of the letter "r".

MARINKA: Ask hov much she charges and ven it can begin.

LULE: Marinka comes from Bosnia and has some problems with pronunciation. She always says hov much, not how much.

MARINKA: How. How. How.

BUD: *(cautiously)* Tell me when will you come, tell me *quando, quando, quando*.[6] Tell me how much will you charge, tell me *quanto, quanto, quanto*.

SHANTI: Shh, stop it! Lule, tell lady well where house is.

LULE: Shanti has problems with articles and verbs. Would you come here?… Great. Do you have something to write it down?… Via Ungaretti 25.… Yes, in old city.

MARINKA: Tell her that it is the pink run-down house, all higgledy-piggledy. Zat with the broken doorway.

LULE: The house is mauve. The elevator is out of use at this moment. Today?… *(She turns to ask the others for confirmation. They say OK.)* Great. We are going to a funeral right now. Our landlord has passed away, but 3 o'clock will be fine. See you later, thank you.

MARINKA: Hov much does she vont?

LULE: Twelve euro. I have to go home to get my hat and sunglasses. Let's meet down at the door in a while? *(She leaves.)*

MARINKA: *Sranje!*[7] Bobo'll kill me if I tell him. Twelve euro!

BUD: 12 divided by 4.

SHANTI: Let's hope!… Well, should I go change?

MARINKA: Why you always listen to her? Not everyone has money to throw away on clothes and designer handbags! Plus, dead people can't see.

LULE: *(off stage)* Hey! Hurry up, girls!

MARINKA: And dead people aren't in hurry!

---

6. Lyrics from the popular song "Quando quando quando" by Tony Renis (1962).

7. Bosnian-Croatian-Serbian, "shit."

Shanti: But Zacchigna was a good man.

Marinka: Man? He wasn't a man, he was a mincer. The first time he shook my hand was like to put it into a mixer! Good, indeed! He was a thief! All off the books and look what a house!

Bud: But rent isn't high. You don't look at the teeth of horse with gifts.

Shanti: He had a good heart for renting the house to foreigners.

Marinka: House! You mean hovel!

Bud: But we've done thousand renovations. And paid from our own pocket.

Shanti: What can you find for two hundred euros today?

Bud: Husbands did lot. Bobo repaired staircase. Fong and Ashok fixed pipes.

Marinka: In all these years only one couple — Lule and Besim — they didn't do anything besides give instructions.

Lule: *(off stage)* Are you all ready or not?… It's not good to arrive late. *(Agitated choir of women complaining about Lule.)*

Mr. Rosso: *(off stage)* Darkies! Be quiet! Always *scandàl,* confusion from morning until night. I can't sleep!

Shanti: He's still sleeping?

Marinka: He always sleeps. He sleeps, reads, smokes and yells.

The First Lesson with Laura

Lule: Nice to meet you, ma'am. I am Mrs. Dardini, the one that called you.

Marinka: Marinka.

BUD: My Chinese name Meiguei. It means bud of a rose so everyone call me Bud.

SHANTI: My name Shanti Kumar. From India.

LAURA: And I'm Laura. I'm *patocca.*

MARINKA: *(perplexed)* In the paper didn't you write that you were Italian?

BUD: Where you from?

LULE: Stop making fools of yourselves. It means that she is a pure blooded Triestine.

LAURA: Yes, sorry, I use a lot of words in dialect. But one can't live in this city if one doesn't know it.

EVERYONE: We noticed.

LAURA: So, how shall we proceed? How about each one introduces the friend sitting on her right?

MARINKA: I start?… Lule comes from Albania. She has three kids that are over there. Her husband is an engineer, and Lule also has degree in something, I don't remember vat.

LULE: Business Management.

MARINKA: Right. Lule is more educated than all of us. She knows how to dress right, talk right, decorate right. The rest of us don't know shit.

LULE: Rose Bud works at the Golden Dragon with her husband. She always dresses with taste and elegance thanks to the cousin that has a shop in Via Ghega, downtown.

BUD: Shanti has very beautiful name. Name in India has meaning like in China. Shanti means peace. She one of my peace friends!

SHANTI: My friend Marinka come from Bosnia, but she never want to talk about her home!

LULE: So if you want to be her friend, talk about everything besides her country. She's married to Bobo, and they have two children, Peter and Dragan.

SHANTI: They are good friends with my daughter Kamla.

LAURA: Well, I see that each one has some little problems, however, I want to congratulate you. But if I am not being a nosy parker, why do you care to learn Italian so well?

SHANTI: To not just say "good morning," "good night," "how much carrot and celery costs?" To speak from heart.

LULE: To emancipate us. After all, integration passes through interaction.

MARINKA: To not hear people always say to me that I am *"sciava"*[8]!

BUD: To say well *(She takes a deep breath.)* rice with red turnips.

LULE: To learn Italian also means to be more aware also of our rights.

MARINKA: We don't have rights. We are foreign. We have only responsibilities. We are immigrants, not princesses on the bean.

LAURA: Pea. But beans are fine just the same. Now maybe I'll explain to you how I would proceed, then you tell me if it's OK you. If you ask me, learning a language isn't enough. You need to learn the culture of the city you live in. So I will also give you practical assignments to perform.

LULE: What do you mean?

8. Triestine dialect, meaning both "slave," and "Slav."

Laura: For example, I'll invite you to go to the theatre, to attend the *osmizze*[9] on the Karst Plateau, the festivals…

Shanti: To become like pukka people of Trieste.

Marinka: In short, complain if *"Capo in B"* coffee[10] isn't vith correct foam. And vere do ve find the money for all zeese things?

Bud: And the time? Restaurant is closed only Wednesday.

Lule: I find it a rather splendid idea! *Dum vivimus, vivamus,* while we live, let us live.

Bud: What did she say?

Marinka: She is already starting *a cagar fuori dal bucal,* bloody show off.[11] I can't stand her.

Laura: Good. Do we want to start by hearing your impressions of Trieste?

Mr. Rosso: *(off stage)* Darkies! Be silent! Damn those who allowed you into this country! Dear me! *(The women laugh.)*

Marinka: He's the only Italian in the building.

Bud: He smoke, drink, get pissed off with darkies and do like Trieste motto: *viva là e pum pum!*[12]

Shanti: His name is Cazzo Altrinegri…. His real name is Alberto Rosso, but when I moved in, he opened the door in his pajamas.

---

9. A form of farmer's market that is traditional in the Karst region.

10. One of the ways one orders coffee in Trieste: "Capo" is short for "cappuccino"; in B stands for "in bicchiere" (in glass).

11. Triestine dialect, "to shit out of the chamber pot." It is said of people acting with arrogance and disregard for their own limits.

12. Bud misquotes a popular Triestine saying, "Viva là e po' bon!" which expresses a carefree attitude. It dates back to the time of Austro-Hungarian rule, when the saying was "Viva l'A e po' bon" (long live A[ustria], and then everything's fine).

He stared at me and yelled: *Cazzo, altri negri!…* I didn't know Italian good and I said: "Good day. I am Shanti Kumar. We will live on the third floor. Nice to meet you Mr. Cazzo Altrinegri." I did not know he means Bloody hell more darkies. I think this his name.

Marinka: From that moment on he steered clear of her, and Shanti named him Cazzo Altrinegri.

Lule: Instead he discussed philosophy at length with my husband when they met on the stairs. I still wasn't so familiar with him.

Marinka: Of course, he hates women!

Lule: However, one day he broke the leg so I thought I'd bring him something to eat. And he started to yell.

Marinka: *(imitating Mr. Rosso)* Go away, friggin' Jehovah's Witnesses!

Lule: I said: "I'm your neighbor, the engineer's wife."

Marinka: *(imitating Mr. Rosso)* What do you want? Scram, darkie!

Lule: In the end he opened the door. And mamma mia, what confusion! What a mess! I said I was also going to clean his place.

Marinka: He thought she wanted to trick him, get close, and then steal his pension.

Lule: He was incredulous. But in the end my modus operandi worked. He gobbled up the soup in the blink of an eye!

Shanti: Instead with my daughter…

Laura: And what with your daughter?

Marinka: Oh yes, with her daughter…

Kamla Meets Mr. Rosso

(Kamla is outside Mr. Rosso's door. He opens it suddenly.)

Kamla: *(singing, with the help of the other women)* We Three Kings from Orient are…

Mr. Rosso: But you are alone. You need to sing I am a king, or better, I am a pain in the neck. Where are the others?

Kamla: Dragan and Peter? They're hiding. They're scared of you.

Mr. Rosso: And you're not?

Kamla: No. I have my magic wand! It can turn you into a toad.

Mr. Rosso: Oh really? But I'm already a toad. I'm mean and I eat kids that are nuisances!

Kamla: You aren't mean. You're just old and alone.

Mr. Rosso: And who told you that?

Kamla: My mamma.

Mr. Rosso: What's your name?

Kamla: Kamla.

Mr. Rosso: Camilla. Well, at least you don't have a darkie name. Come on, sing. You will probably sing better than the darkies at Sanremo, they're only there because they have friends in high places. But don't think I'll give you money for it.

Kamla: Give a euro to Peter. He wants to buy a yo-yo.

Mr. Rosso: A good smack is what I'm going to give to that coward who left you here all by yourself. How old are you?

Kamla: I'm five. You can be my friend even if you're poor.

Mr. Rosso: Your friend? Do you know how old I am?

Kamla: No.

Mr. Rosso: I could be your grandfather.

Kamla: My grandparents are in Dhaka.

Mr. Rosso: It's better that they stay there. We don't need more darkies, right?

Kamla: Right.

Mr. Rosso: Do you like poetry?

Kamla: Yes.

Mr. Rosso: Do you know Ungaretti?

Kamla: Yes.

Mr. Rosso: Really? Let's hear what you know by Ungaretti.

Kamla: Via Ungaretti 25. That's where I live.

Mr. Rosso: Nice one! Would you like to learn poetry?

Kamla: Yes.

Shanti: Kamla, what are you doing? Don't bother gentleman.

Mr. Rosso: No, she's not bothering me at all. Actually, I would like to ask — would you send her to my place every once in a while so that she can learn poetry?

Shanti: I have to ask husband. I beg your pardon, you got letter?

Mr. Rosso: Letter? Ah, that letter? Yes, I threw it away. I don't give a damn. They don't scare me. Why? Did you get scared?

Shanti: Yes.

Mr. Rosso: Ah, I thought you darkies had more balls than that because of everything you had to go through to get here. Instead you're shitting your pants for nothing. *(Closes the door. Leaves.)*

Kamla: Can I go visit him, mamma?

Shanti: *(says a sentence in Hindi)* We'll see, Marinka says he is a faxist.

Kamla: What's faxist?

Shanti: Someone who hates foreigners. We'll ask dad tonight.

Continuation

Narrator's Voice: The months passed, and Bud learned little by little how to pronounce the letter "r." Marinka managed to say "when" instead of "ven," and Shanti absorbed the fact that the phrase "to be as cunning as an Indian" has nothing to do with her own people. And Lule, well, Lule showed off her Latin and her pretty clothes.

Five women, four foreigners and one Italian, learned to mix grammar and feelings.

But for the foreigners there was no end to the surprises.

Rose Bud asked why in Italian one says "*amiche per la pelle*" — literally "friends for the skin" — to mean "friends for life." In Chinese it seems that there's a similar expression that translates as "friends for the bones."

Marinka suggested changing the Italian expression to "friends for the wardrobe," because Italians judge you fundamentally on how you dress.

Shanti was frequently discouraged, accusing Italian of being a deliberately difficult language in order to thwart integration.

The ladies learned the subjunctive, but also women's rights. I, too, learned many things from them. I learned that emancipation is neither a unique nor a universal concept. In many latitudes to be able to carve out a little space to take Italian lessons is in itself an achievement.

Kamla in the meantime brought a little springtime to a man in the winter of his life.

(Kamla and Rosso are seen reading from a book of poetry.)

Christmas

Bud: Mamma mia, a year's gone by already! It feels so strange.

Marinka: You know what's really strange? None of us is Catholic, and we're celebrating Christmas.

Shanti: None of us is Italian, and we're speaking Italian.

Bud: We've become *"batocche"*[13] like Laura.

Marinka: *(laughing) Patocche.* Local. Even if I do feel a bit *batocca* now that I've heard the latest. Don't you know? They're coming on Monday to do the site inspection for our eviction.

Lule: Come on, let's not talk about it today — it's Christmas.

Marinka: Certainly she's not worried! She has plenty of money. Like that Mr. Cazzo Altrinegri. The Fongs, too, are full of *bori,* rolling in dough. Shanti, it's only the two of us that are going to have to queue up at Montuzza for a bowl of soup. *(The women start to set out the food.)*

Lule: I brought some canapés: salmon and shrimp.

Bud: I made spring rolls.

---

13. Bud confuses *batòca* (Venetian dialect: thrashing, blow) with *patocca* (plural: *patocche*), which is how Laura had described herself, a full-blooded Triestine. Hence Marinka's pun, "I feel a little *batocca* (thrashed, beaten up, bloodied) myself now that I've heard the latest."

Marinka: *Mi gò portà questo,* I brought this. It needs to be warmed for two minutes. *(Shanti smells a strange smell and moves closer to the plate.)*

Shanti: What is it?

Lule: *Jota,*[14] I think.

Marinka: Try it, Shanti. The sauerkraut is really strong because I didn't rinse it. I also put a little *cotica* in it.

Bud: What is *cotica*?

Marinka: Pig skin.

Shanti: I don't eat pigs!

Marinka: Well then just eat the beans.

Shanti: I can't.

Bud: I can't either.

Lule: I'll have some later. I'm not hungry right now.

Marinka: Ok, I get it. You don't feel like eating it. I spent four hours cooking for nothing....

Shouldn't this have been a dinner of integration? We talked about making typical food. You know what I think? You'll never integrate!

Shanti: But can't we start to integrate with desserts? *Putizza, presnitz, fave.*[15]

---

14. *Jota* — a sauerkraut and bean stew very popular in Trieste and the Friuli Venezia Giulia region — shows the prominent Austrian influence on the region's cuisine.

15. *Putizza* (*potica* in Slovenian), a sweet roll with any of a variety of fillings, is an example of Slovenian-Italian-Jewish fusion. *Presnitz* (named after the Slovenian Easter cake *presnec* and similar to a strudel) is a spiral of puff-pastry filled with nuts, dried fruit, and spices. *Fave* (or *fave dei morti*, beans of the

Marinka: You know what I think? If you can't even digest this soup, how do you intend to digest life in this country? *(She leaves, slamming the door.)*

The Last Lesson with Laura

(The friends are reading the classifieds in Il Piccolo, *Trieste's daily paper.)*

Bud: Via Paisiello. Eighty-seven thousand euro. For active people. What do they mean, "active people"?

Marinka: That there are only stairs.

Bud: So why don't they write "without an elevator"?

Marinka: Don't you know that they don't ever say what they mean? *(Laura enters.)*

Laura: Guys! Good news! I've managed to score some tickets for the operetta. There's *Elisabeth* next Wednesday. You remember the lesson that we had about Sissi[16] after the visit to Miramare castle?

Bud: I really liked Princess Carlotta's Chinese room!

Shanti: I asked: how many servants did she have?

Marinka: Did you notice that back then all the women were tiny and had mustaches? Shame that I hadn't been born that instant! However, we can't come.

Shanti: For a long time we were wanting to tell you that… that… this is the last lesson.

---

dead) are macaroon-like almond cookies made, with some regional variations, throughout Italy for All Saints Day and All Souls Day. These desserts illustrate how traditional local specialties are the result of culinary migrations and interminglings.

16. Empress Elisabeth of Austria.

Bud: In three weeks we have to leave Via Ungaretti.

Lule: The official eviction letter arrived yesterday.

Marinka: Read.

Laura: To Whom It May Concern. This is to inform you that, following the death of Mr. Zacchigna Enrico, his only heir Zacchigna Mauro invites you to vacate the apartment...yada yada yada.... But it says here that this story has gone on for a year! Why didn't you all tell me before?

Shanti: You already have a lot of problems.

Marinka: We thought it was just an excuse to increase rent.

Lule: Through his contacts my husband thought he could resolve the situation.

Bud: We told the new landlord that he's asking too much for the price. This place is in scrambles.[17]

Laura: In scrambles?

Lule: In shambles.

Bud: Also bosses from restaurant Golden Dragon made pre-emptive offer.

Marinka: The only good thing is that we've learned a lot of Italian in these months. Now I can be lawyer's secretary.

Shanti: Now I know what they mean when they say "unauthorized."

Marinka: It's worse than "darkie" and "illegal." But did we have a choice? Even Cazzo Altrinegri is off the books.

Laura: Are you sure you did everything you could?

---

17. In the original, Bud confuses "catapecchia" (hovel) with "cartapesta" (papier-mâché).

LULE: Yes, everything. There isn't anything to do. Next week they're coming to put the seals on.

SHANTI: We found very small apartment in the outskirts.

LULE: We've decided to go back to Albania.

BUD: I hope, hope, hope to have good news soon…

SHANTI: Laura, the day after tomorrow we're having a farewell dinner. We would like it if you come…to come…could come!

LAURA: Good job. "Could come." I have a protest organized by the Friends of San Giacomo's Linden Trees, they want to chop them down, but I'll stop by. I'm sorry that I can't do anything, but if this house is uninhabitable, there isn't much you can do.

SHANTI: It's taken me years to try and understand this country. Why shoes cost more than refrigerator?

MARINKA: Why they're obsessed with a tan, specially the old people.

BUD: Why people like Rosso spend half pension feeding stray cats with cans of Whiskas.

SHANTI: But what I really can't understand is the word "uninhabitable." If we stay how can it be uninhabitable?

THE TRUTH ABOUT LULE IS DISCOVERED

(Marinka and Shanti are alone.)

MARINKA: Shanti, Shanti, you will not believe your ears. Lule is not who you think she is!

SHANTI: What do you mean?

MARINKA: No! She's not a grand lady full of money. She's a servant like me!

Shanti: What are you saying.

Marinka: I swear! I've seen her with my own eyes! She was in the bathroom cleaning behind the crapper at the house of the new lady where I go to clean Tuesdays. *(The bell rings. Lule enters, disheveled. She has been crying.)*

Lule: She's already told you everything, right?

Marinka: So it was all rubbish. The big villa back home, Besim's cool job…

Lule: The house was there. It was taken during the dictatorship. Because of this we escaped from there. Besim was an engineer in Albania, but his degree was not accepted here, and he hasn't found a job. He is only a volunteer for Caritas. I am the one who supports the family.

Shanti: But all your dresses?

Lule: The lady I clean for gives me the ones she no longer wears.

Marinka: And the story of your kids? Is that also rubbish?

Lule: They're… they're in foster care because we couldn't… did not manage to… I was ashamed to tell the truth.

Shanti: Shh, don't cry! You were scared of what we'd think?

Lule: I didn't know how to tell you. What you would have thought of me…

Shanti: But are we or are we not friends for life?

Laura Narrates: The women have organized a going-away party. Farewells are sad, but they're also moments of profound understanding and of intense truth. The last spoonful of pudding is always the sweetest.

Marinka has confessed why she had never wanted to talk about the past, always saying that the only verb tense that interested her was the future. She has explained the drama of losing her house and her family during the war.

Obviously, we had sensed it. A friend listens to what you say, but a real friend understands especially what you don't say. We five had become true friends, "friends for the liver," as Shanti said, translating from Hindi.

I had to leave — I had a reunion for the safeguard of the bees of Val Rosandra, but I needed to say goodbye to Bud.

She finally came in, excited, singing at the top of her lungs.

Bud: *Vincerò, vincerò, vinceeeero!*[18] We have won!

Marinka: Have you been drinking?

Bud: We won't leave! We won't move! The owners of Golden Dragon bought all the building!

The Others: *(chorus of excited voices, celebrations and music)* Really?... Are you kidding?... Is it for real?... Via Ungaretti?... How come?

Some Time Later

Shanti: Another funeral!

Lule: Poor Mr. Rosso. He died from preoccupation and heartbreak. He thought he would have to leave Via Ungaretti. It's a shame he didn't get to know the good news that we won't be evicted! But what a man! He has kept us in the dark all this time!

Marinka: Who would have thought it! Our very own Cazzo Altrinegri had a love story with a black woman!

Lule: And what a story!

18. Lyrics from "Nessun dorma," a famous aria from the final act of Giacomo Puccini's opera *Turandot.*

Shanti: It seems like Indian movie!

Bud: Can you tell me what you are talking about?

Lule: At the end of the thirties, he was in Ethiopia, where he met a local woman. He couldn't marry her because of racial laws, though. They had a girl called Anita. She's apparently his only heir, isn't she?

Marinka: You miss Mr. Rosso, don't you, Kamla?

Kamla: Yes.

Lule: What do you have there?

Kamla: A poem. I found it under the door.

Shanti: Read, Kamla. *(Kamla runs towards Mr. Rosso, who appears as though in a dream. They hug each other. Kamla sits on his knees and they recite together.)*

Mr. Rosso:

Will and Verse[19]

The December of life
Knocks on my door
So here are my wishes
For when I am no more.

My January of joy
The first month of year
Can be no one else
But Anita my dear
To whom I leave all.

February
So cold
And I'm not the proprietor
Of my household.

19. The English version of the poem was provided by the author.

Crazy old March
Let it go
Forget it has thirty-one days
In a row.

April
Herald of spring
And to my reawakening
Camilla
I wish to bequeath
All my books – both messy and neat.

(When Kamla hears the word "Camilla" she repeats it, surprised.)

KAMLA: It's me, mamma!

MR. ROSSO:

The next few months
Are times of toil
Some work selflessly
Some for the spoil.

Weeds like me
Need to be plucked
By a gentle hand
Who will always understand
That to reap
You need to sow
And to judge
You need to know.

For friendship
And tender care
Thanks to all of Via Ungaretti
For always being there.

The old man's dead
Tell the pastor not to preach
And as for my neighbours
I leave them twenty thousand scillini *each.*

November so tender
And my cats so dear
Twenty thousand for them too
So they have nothing to fear.

And remember me not
As only mean and mad
This is a last will and testament
Though the poetry be bad

Lucidly yours,
Alberto Rosso

Marinka: *Sranje!* It's a will. So, it's for us?

Bud: *Scillini?* It's a shame shillings is no used now.

Marinka: It's an expression, silly! Like ven he called you *mania gatti,* cat eater,[20] but deep inside he must have cared about you. Or he wouldn't leave you all zees money, right.

Shanti: We can resume lessons with Laura.

Bud: Yeah, great! Come on, Lule. You call her.

Lule: Ms. Laura, good morning, it is Lule. Do you remember the four good friends?

All the Women: Gutsy friends!

Lule: …we would like to resume the Italian lessons.

All the Women: *(chorus of excited voices)* On Wednesday, restaurant is closed. Here, here. Ask how much she vont.

20. *Mania gatti* (commonly spelled *magnagati* or *magna gatti*), meaning "cat eater(s)," is a nickname traditionally used for people of Vicenza, a city in the neighboring Veneto region. In the narrative version of *Amiche per la pelle*, Mr. Rosso uses this epithet when he unjustifiably blames Bud and her family for the disappearance of some of his feline friends.

Yousef Wakkas

Cherry Kebab and Strawberry Lasagna[1]

The ladies of the house were not inclined to question their certitude. I might indeed be nourished by delicious dishes abroad, but no dish could ever compare to Cherry Kebab. And besides, we were in peak season, and the only thing left to decide was if they should choose *Rihawi* cherries or our local ones. Local of course meaning the *Karaz A'zazi,* the cherries of Azaz, my hometown. In the morning, signs of controversy were already stirring in the air, but by afternoon, with the arrival of aunts Lamia' and Nura, things got even more complicated, splitting the women into two clear-cut factions — supporters and dogged opponents.

"Cherry Kebab is only made with *Rihawi* cherries, the way our grandmothers and great-grandmothers did it!"

"So what? Are our cherries perhaps any less good?"

"No, but it's only made with *Rihawi.*"

"That's what you say."

No one asked my opinion, despite the fact that I was, however indirectly, the reason for the discord. About a month had passed since my return, and I still found myself in the role of honored guest: invitations one after the other and special treatment from all my family members, big and small, as if I were he-who-had-conquered-all-of-Europe. At times they embarrassed me to death, and often they spoiled me so much I felt like a source of competition for them. But the thing that saddened me most of all was the fact that I felt like a stranger among them.

1. Yousef Wakkas, "Kebab di ciliege e lasagna alle fragole," in *Mondo pentola,* ed. Laila Wadia (Isernia: Cosmo Iannone, 2007).

"His appearance seems to have changed. He doesn't resemble the person we used to know!" they said secretly, exchanging understanding looks.

They, too, had changed, and some had passed away. I missed my mother a lot. She would have wanted to see me at all costs, they said, shedding tears. The intensity of the commotion increased with the arrival of yet another relative. Then, after a few nostalgic memories, always followed by the same question, "But don't you remember?" they would turn to the inevitable comparison between us and the European countries. Some maintained that we are better, and others asserted that, with respect to them, we are living in the stone age. One day, however, while I was watching a documentary on Rai Utile,[2] both one side and the other had to backpedal, saying almost in unison, "So they're just like us?!" The *trulli*[3] that jutted into the blue sky seemed like those we had in neighboring villages, with the sole exception that in Alberobello the streets were clean and neat, while in our villages, such order was pretty much lacking. But what attracted their attention more than anything else was the grandmother who was preparing pasta in her own home, surrounded by her daughter-in-law and some grandchildren.

"It's just the same as here. She's making *Shish Barak* (equivalent to *cappelletti*)."

"But they add eggs to the dough — it must be tastier."

I had to explain everything to them, from the significance of maintaining tradition to the smallest details relating to the doughs and the sauces. That same day they forced me to prepare a large pot of pasta with pesto sauce! They thanked the people of Genoa

2. Rai Utile was an interactive television channel that transmitted over digital terrestrial television by satellite and in streaming video through the Rai-TV website from January 2004 to January 2008.

3. Traditional dry stone huts with conical roofs, specific to the Itria Valley of Puglia.

for this invention, and I took the opportunity to reveal to them that it was Christopher Columbus' favorite dish, since he was full-blooded Genoese.

"You mean he wasn't Spanish?"

"No."

"But the ships were Spanish."

"Yes."

"And he ate pasta with pesto sauce throughout the entire journey?"

"Yes."

"Only pesto?"

"Only."

"Incredible!"

The children's curiosity fired up with each of my revelations. The grown-ups were no less curious, but they were much more interested in learning about me than about the great conquests of men, while at the same time dragging me back into the past, or in other words, reintegrating me. And in their opinion, that process passed first through the stomach. From this idea was born their insistence on traditional dishes.

Anyway, the heated discussion blew over by late afternoon, when the midwife, an elderly woman of Circassian descent who lived in a small house close to the Armenian cemetery, came by to visit us.

"I brought you into the world, you know," were Mrs. Bashira's first words, while she took her place on the *kravit,* a chest of drawers set along the wall in front of the windows that overlooked the courtyard and was covered with colorful cushions that reached to the floor, the kind that doubles as a sofa and as a storage space for odds and ends. My father's military uniform had been lying there since 1948.

"Yes," I nodded, feigning a diffidence suitable to the occasion.

"You made us suffer a lot, almost two days. Then you were born at dawn, and your father called the gypsies to celebrate. Three days of drums and dances. And then you left us, and your mother… ahh…the poor thing! She wasn't able to see you."

And everyone started to cry. This by now had become a normal sight ever since I set foot in the house.

"Grandmother, enough with the tears. It's five o'clock. It's time to get dinner," intervened Aunt Lamia', appropriately nicknamed *Battleaxe.*

"And what do you want from me," asked Grandmother Bashira, drying her tears.

"We want to make Cherry Kebab for Suleyman, and we can't agree whether we should use *Rihawi* or local cherries," said my older sister, making a gesture with her head as if to say "Here we go again."

"Nonsense!" Grandmother Bashira exclaimed. "Ours are sweet as syrup. Girls, Cherry Kebab is only made with amarena cherries, for their tartness."

"That's what I told them, but no one wanted to listen to me," Aunt Nura said triumphantly.

"There are many kinds of cherry, and Cherry Kebab is only made with amarena cherries," Grandmother Bashira clarified.

Then she continued as if she were in front of the burner stirring the dish: "So, first of all you wash the amarena cherries really well, and you get the juice by crushing them against a fine sieve."

"We have a blender, grandmother," my younger sister interrupted.

"In my day, we didn't use a blender," Grandmother Bashira replied in exasperation. "Women today don't want to work hard! Anyway, do what you want. Next the ground meat is seasoned with salt, pepper, cinnamon, and pine nuts. You make little meatballs and fry them with butter. The cherry juice cooks in a pan with sugar added to taste. Usually we add fifty grams of sugar for every glass of juice. When the sauce is reduced, you add in the little meatballs and let them boil in the gravy for about five minutes. In a separate serving dish — glass is better — you place small pieces of toasted bread and then you pour the kebab over it, sprinkling it with finely chopped parsley and a little ground cinnamon."

"We don't use cinnamon," observed Aunt Nura.

"Well then, sprinkle a little black pepper! You know nothing about this!" replied Grandmother Bashira reproachfully.

Tradition was nevertheless well respected. The decrees of the elders were followed to the letter. In fact, right after Grandmother Bashira's epilogue, the women rushed into the kitchen. There was also, however, the usual hubbub of old times. The radio was set at high volume, and the voice of the singer was mixed with the noises of the pots and the racket of the kids who were playing under the trees. Immersed in pleasant thoughts, I saw my childhood pass before my eyes. Right there, under the pomegranate tree, I once played, too, and like them, I tried to expend my energy by every possible means, even leaping over the flowerbeds from one side to the other like the athletes I saw at the town sports ground.

I was about to tell one of my nephews another tall tale, when at that moment they announced that dinner was served. We all gathered around the tablecloth of waxed canvas spread in the hall that divides the guest room from the living room. I wasn't used to sitting on the floor anymore, but I had to adapt. Everyone ate quietly, ears perked up. Finally Aunt Nura couldn't stand it any longer.

"So, you like it?"

"Yes."

"I've prepared a surprise for you!"

"What kind of surprise?"

There was an expectant silence. Everyone had stopped eating and stared at me intently.

"You remember that recipe you wrote down for me?"

"Which one?"

I had written more than one recipe.

"The…*latsania*."

"Lasagna?"

"Yes, that one!"

"What of it?"

"I made a pan of it…but…not the way the Italians make it. I've made it tastier!"

"What do you mean?"

Some people were already doubled up with laughter.

"Come on! Bring it out!" urged my older sister.

Aunt Nura got up all of a sudden and like a hurricane sweeping away everything in its path, knocking over jugs of water, slippers, and stools, she went into the kitchen and returned holding in her hands a steaming pan.

"Look!" she said anxiously. "Strawberry *latsania!*"

She wanted to surprise me, and she had succeeded completely.

I was stunned at the sight before me: the servings of lasagna, already cut into squares, were garnished with giant strawberries, and their contrasting fragrance mingled strongly with the aromas of ragú and béchamel!

About the Authors

Ubah Cristina Ali Farah was born in 1973 in Verona, Italy, of a Somali father and an Italian mother. She grew up in Mogadishu, Somalia, but fled at the outbreak of the civil war at the age of eighteen, moving first to Hungary and then to Italy. She received a Ph.D. in African Studies from the University of Naples-L'Orientale with a dissertation on Somali popular culture and lived in Rome where she taught Somali language and culture at Roma Tre University. She is currently based in Brussels.

Ali Farah is a poet, novelist, playwright, and oral performer. She is the author of two novels set in Italy and dealing with two generations of Somali refugees: *Madre piccola* (Segrate (MI): Frassinelli, 2007), which won the Vittorini Prize, and *Il Comandante del fiume* (Rome: 66thand2nd, 2014). She has published short stories and poems in numerous journals, including *Caffè*, *Crocevia*, *El Ghibli*, *Nuovi Argomenti*, *Quaderni del 900*, *Pagine*, and *Sagarana*, and in anthologies such as *Ai confini del verso: Poesia della migrazione in italiano,* ed. Mia Lecomte (Milan: Le Lettere, 2006). She has also contributed to several newspapers and periodicals, including *Internazionale*, *Il Sole 24 Ore*, *Nigrizia*, *Repubblica*, and "The Black Blog" of *Vogue Italia*. Ali Farah won the 2006 Lingua Madre national literary competition.

Her novel *Madre piccola* has been translated into Dutch as *Barni en Domenica* (Amsterdam: Sirene, 2008), and into English as *Little Mother* (Bloomington: Indiana University Press, 2011). English translations of her work have appeared in the following journals and anthologies: *Metamorphoses* (Spring and Fall 2006); *A New Map: The Poetry of Migrant Writers in Italy,* ed. Mia Lecomte and Luigi Bonaffini (Ottawa: Legas, 2011); and *Banthology: Stories from Banned Nations,* ed. Sarah Cleave (Dallas: Deep Vellum, 2018).

Clementina Sandra Ammendola was born in Buenos Aires in 1963 to an Argentine mother of Spanish and Italian origin and an Italian father who emigrated from Calabria in the 1950s. After receiving a degree in Sociology, she moved to Italy in 1989, at the time of the Argentine great depression, which fueled the "return migration" of people of Italian ancestry to their paternal or maternal homeland. She currently lives in Turin, where she works as an educator at a community shelter for adolescent girls. She defines herself as a "migrola": a migrant subject, who lives and studies migration out of necessity, and a migrant writer in search of multiple voices and points of view.

Ammendola's poetry received awards in the second and fourth editions of the Literary Award for Migrant Writers Eks&Tra, and one of her short stories received honorable mention in the third edition of the Eks&Tra contest. She also won the 2009 Migrant Literature for Children Award CIES Roma with the short story "Si dice di me," translated in the present anthology. She is the author of the bilingual fictional autobiography *Lei, che sono io — Ella, que soy yo* (Rome: Sinnos, 2005), and has published short stories and poems in various journals and blogs, including *Sagarana, Kúmá, Vibrizze Bollettino,* and *La Bottega del Barbieri.*

Her short stories have been published in the following collections: *Memorie in valigia,* ed. Alessandro Ramberti and Roberta Sangiorgi (Santarcangelo di Romagna (RI): Fara Editore, 1997); *Parole di sabbia,* ed. F. Argento, A. Melandri, and P. Trabucco (Mercato San Severino (SA): Edizioni Il Grappolo, 2002); *Lingua Madre Duemilasei: Racconti di donne straniere in Italia,* ed. Daniela Finocchi (Turin: Edizioni SEB27, 2006); *Mondopentola,* ed. Laila Wadia (Isernia: Cosmo Iannone, 2007); *Sono partito dall'altra parte del libro per incontrarti* (Rome: Sinnos, 2009); and *Roba da donne: Emancipazione e scrittura nei percorsi di autrici dal mondo,* ed. Silvia Camilotti (Rome: Mangrovie Edizioni, 2009).

Paul Bakolo Ngoi was born in Mbandaka, Democratic Republic of the Congo (formerly Zaire) in 1962. He moved to Italy in 1982 and earned a degree in Political Science in Pavia, his adoptive city, where he still lives and works as a cultural mediator and freelance journalist. In addition to Lingala and Italian, he speaks French and English. Bakolo Ngoi inherited his passion for traveling from his father, a former diplomat, and his vocation as a writer from his paternal grandfather, a noted griot in his homeland. He often finds inspiration for his stories in the oral tradition of his tribe.

Bakolo Ngoi was one of the winners of the first edition of the Eks&Tra Award for Migrant Writers (1995) and was conferred an honorable mention in the fourth edition of the contest (1998) for narrative entries that included "Una lezione a metà," translated in the present anthology. He is best known for his contributions to children's literature. *Colpo di testa* (Milan: Fabbri Editori, 2003), his most successful book, won the Gino Perrone Città di San Donato di Lecce Award (2003) and the Città di Bella Award for Children's Literature (2005). It has been translated into French and Korean.

Other publications include: *Un tiro in porta per lo stregone* (Milan: Africa '70, 1994); *Che vita sia! (Una storia per i grandi), Eko, color cioccolato e Koba la tartaruga (Una storia per i piccoli)* (Milan: Autocircuito, 2006); *Magia nera a Kinshasa* (Milan: Edizioni dell'Arco, 2006); *Chi ha mai sentito russare una banana?* (Milan: Fabbri Editori, 2007), translated in Spanish and Korean; *Corri Lidja, corri* (Rome: Edizioni Paoline, 2010); *Una sorpresa per Babbo Natale* (Kinshasa: Lokole d'Afrik, 2010); and *Dov'è finito Babbo Natale* (Kinshasa: Lokole d'Afrik, 2012).

Mihai Mircea Butcovan was born in Oradea, in Transylvania, Romania, in 1969, and has lived in Italy since 1991. He currently resides in Sesto San Giovanni and works in Milan as an educator in the fields of substance abuse and intercultural communication, collaborating with public and private organizations, schools, libraries, and cultural centers. He is a member of the editorial board of the online periodical of migration literature *El Ghibli* and contributes to various other journals, including *Internazionale*, *il manifesto*, and *Caposud*.

Butcovan is the author of a novel, *Allunaggio di un immigrante innamorato* (Nardò (LE): Besa, 2006), which won the Voci Migranti Prize, and two collections of poems: *Borgo Farfalla* (San Giovanni in Persiceto (BO): Eks&Tra, 2006), which won a prize at the twelfth edition of the Literary Award for Migrant Writers Eks&Tra, and *Dal comunismo al consumismo* (Ferrara: La Carmelina, 2009).

His poems and short stories have appeared in the journals *Pagine*, *Sagarana*, *Kúmá*, and *El Ghibli*, as well as in several anthologies: *Nuovo Planetario Italiano: Geografia e antologia della letteratura della migrazione in Italia e in Europa,* ed. Armando Gnisci (Troina (EN): Città Aperta, 2006); *Ai confini del verso: Poesia della migrazione in italiano,* ed. Mia Lecomte (Milan: Le Lettere, 2006); *Sapori Incontri Fragranze,* ed. L. Dugulin and M. Richter (Trieste: Cacit, 2006); *San Nicola: Agiografia immaginaria,* ed. M. Lobaccaro and R. Kubati (Molfetta (BA): La meridiana, 2006); *Il carro di pickipò,* ed. P. Gavagna and R. Taddeo (Rome: Ediesse, 2006); *Mondopentola,* ed. Laila Wadia (Isernia: Cosmo Iannone, 2007); and *Pubblichiamoli a casa loro: Prove letterarie di umorismo migrante,* ed. Matteo Andreone and Raffaele Taddeo (Rome: Ensemble, 2018). A selection of his poems has been translated into English in *A New Map: The Poetry of Migrant Writers in Italy,* ed. Mia Lecomte and Luigi Bonaffini (Ottawa: Legas, 2011).

Rosana Crispim da Costa was born in 1966 in São Paulo, Brazil. She lives with her family in Sant'Agata Feltria (Rimini), a municipality in the Italian region Emilia-Romagna. She is the author of three collections of poetry: *Il mio corpo traduce molte lingue* (Santarcangelo di Romagna (RI): Fara Editore, 1998; also published in Brazil as *O Meu Corpo Trazuz Muitas Linguas* (Guaraginguetá: Penalux, 2015); *Desejo* (San Giovanni in Persiceto (BO): Eks&Tra, 2006); and *Tra mura di vento* (Patti (ME): Centro Studi Tindari Patti, 2010).

Her work has been published in numerous anthologies, including: *Memorie in valigia*, ed. Alessandro Ramberti and Roberta Sangiorgi (Santarcangelo di Romagna (RI): Fara Editore, 1997); *Destini sospesi di volti in cammino*, ed. Alessandro Ramberti and Roberta Sangiorgi (Santarcangelo di Romagna (RI): Fara Editore, 1998); *Il doppio sguardo: Culture allo specchio* (Rome: Adnkronos, 2002); *Lingua Madre Duemilasei*, ed. Daniela Finocchi (Turin: Edizioni SEB27, 2006); *Lingua Madre Duemilasette*, ed. Daniela Finocchi (Turin: Edizioni SEB27, 2007); and *Sono partito dall'altra parte del libro per incontrarti* (Rome: Sinnos, 2009).

Among other recognitions, she was awarded first prize for poetry in the 1997 Eks&Tra contest, the 2007 Lingua Madre Literary Prize, the 2009 National Poetry Prize Città di Castorano, the 2010 Literary Prize Scrivere altrove, and the 2011 Literary Prize Diverso ma Uno. Crispim da Costa has contributed to radio and TV programs on current issues. She also works as an intercultural educator and most recently as a songwriter for a number of musicians. In collaboration with the cultural association D'là de' foss, of which she is a co-founding member, she directs a program of poetry and music from around the world, "I Dialetti nelle Valli Del Mondo."

Christiana de Caldas Brito was born in Rio de Janeiro, Brazil, in 1939, and has lived in Rome since 1990. In addition to Brazil and Italy, she has lived one year in the United States, and two years each in Argentina and Austria. She holds degrees in Philosophy, Psychology, and Drama, and practices psychotherapy. She began writing in her native language when she was very young and published stories in Brazilian magazines.

After moving to Rome she adopted Italian as a literary language and achieved her first success with the short story "Ana de Jesus," which won an award in the first edition of the contest for migrant writers organized by the intercultural organization Eks&Tra (1995). The story, first published in the collection *Le voci dell'arcobaleno,* ed. Alessandro Ramberti and Roberta Sangiorgi (Santarcangelo di Romagna (RI): Fara Editore, 1995), was then adapted for the theater and performed throughout Italy. Her subsequent publications include collections of short stories and novels: *Amanda Olinda Azzurra e le altre* (Rome: Lilith, 1998; Nocera: Oèdipus, 2004); *La storia di Adelaide e Marco* (Mercato San Severino (SA): Edizioni Il Grappolo, 2000); *Qui e là* (Isernia: Cosmo Iannone, 2004); *500 temporali* (Isernia: Cosmo Iannone, 2006), and *Colpo di mare* (Arcidosso (GR): Effigi, 2008).

In 2003 her short story collection *Amanda Olinda Azzurra e le altre* won the Award for Writing by Women Il Paese delle donne. Her stories have appeared in numerous journals and anthologies and have been translated into Portuguese, English, French, and German. De Caldas Brito conducts regular workshops in creative writing and has published a handbook based on these experiences, *Viviscrivi: verso il tuo racconto* (San Giovanni in Persiceto (BO): Eks&Tra, 2008). Cultural Institutes in Brazil, Austria, Turkey, and most recently Angola have invited her to talk about her work and to conduct workshops in creative writing.

Amor Dekhis was born in the Sétif Province of Algeria. After completing his studies at the Ècole Nationale des Beaux-Arts in Algiers, he moved to Florence to attend the Istituto Superiore per le Industrie Artistiche, from which he graduated in 1988 with a specialization in Industrial Design. He resides in Florence, where he works as a painter and industrial designer. Dekhis is the author of numerous short stories and two novels: *I lupi della notte* (Naples: L'Ancora del Mediterraneo, 2008), which was a finalist for the Italo Calvino Prize and won the Popoli in cammino Prize, and *Dopotutto ognuno è solo* (Florence: Barbera, 2013).

His short stories have appeared in journals such as *Caffè*, *NarraSud*, and *Sagarana*, as well as in many anthologies: *Le voci dell'arcobaleno*, ed. Alessandro Ramberti and Roberta Sangiorgi (Santarcangelo di Romagna (RI): Fara Editore, 1995); *Mosaici d'inchiostro*, ed. Roberta Sangiorgi (Santarcangelo di Romagna (RI): Fara Editore, 1996); *Memorie in valigia*, ed. Alessandro Ramberti and Roberta Sangiorgi (Santarcangelo di Romagna (RI): Fara Editore, 1997); *Destini sospesi di volti in cammino,* ed. Alessandro Ramberti and Roberta Sangiorgi (Santarcangelo di Romagna (RI): Fara Editore, 1998); *Voci migranti*, ed. Grazia Naletto (Rome: Lunaria, 2000); *Anime in viaggio: La nuova mappa dei popoli* (Rome: Adnkronos, 2001); *Matriciana/Cuscus: Storie d'integrazione* (Padova: Poligrafo, 2002); *Saudade,* ed. N. Giacomo (Milan: Bevivino, 2003); and *Impronte: Scritture dal mondo* (Nardò (LE): Besa, 2003).

His short story "La salvezza," winner of the Matriciana cuscus Award, has been translated into English in *Multicultural Literature in Contemporary Italy,* ed. Marie Orton and Graziella Parati (Madison, NJ: Fairleigh Dickinson University Press, 2007). He was awarded honorable mention in the second, third and fourth editions of the Eks&Tra Award for Migrant Writers (1996, 1997, 1998), won the fourth prize in the 2000 edition, and the third prize in the 2003 edition of the contest.

GËZIM HAJDARI was born in 1957 in Lushnjë, Albania. A political activist, journalist, and outspoken critic of the Hoxha regime and the post-Communist government, Hajdari was forced to leave his country amid censorship of his poetry and threats against his life. He has lived in Italy since 1992. He studied Albanian Literature at the A. Xhuvani University in Elbasan and Modern Literature at the La Sapienza University in Rome and has held a variety of jobs in both Albania and Italy, including factory worker, accountant, teacher, stable boy, field hand, and assistant typographer.

Since his debut on the Italian literary scene with *Ombra di cane / Hije qeni* (Frosinone: Dismisura, 1993), Hajdari has published thirteen dual-language collections of poetry. Among his critically acclaimed works are *Antologia della pioggia* (Santarcangelo di Romagna (RI): Fara Editore, 2000), *Stigmate* (Nardò (LE): Besa, 2002), *Spine Nere* (Nardò (LE): Besa, 2004), *Poema dell'esilio* (Santarcangelo di Romagna (RI): Fara Editore, 2005), *Puligòrga* (Nardò (LE): Besa, 2007), *Corpo presente* (Nardò (LE): Besa, 2011), *Nûr: Eresia e besa* (Rome: Ensemble, 2012), and *Delta del tuo fiume* (Rome: Ensemble, 2015). He writes his verses in both Albanian and Italian, through what he describes as a parallel creative practice of linguistic migration between the two languages. He is the director of the "Erranze" series published by the Ensemble press, and president of the Centro Internazionale Eugenio Montale.

His poetry has been translated into English, French, German, Greek, and Spanish. In 1995, he won first prize for poetry at the inaugural edition of the Eks&Tra Award, followed by several other Eks&Tra prizes, and numerous other awards, including the prestigious Montale Prize (1997) and Dario Bellezza Prize (2000). For his literary merits, Hajdari has been granted honorary citizenship of Frosinone, the Italian town south of Rome where he currently lives and works as a translator and editorial consultant.

Pap Khouma was born in 1957 in Dakar, Senegal. He migrated to Abidjan, Ivory Coast, in 1974, and then to Europe in 1984. After a failed attempt to get into Germany and a short stay in France, he settled in Milan where he still lives. During his early years in Italy, he survived as a street vendor. He has since worked as a manual laborer, delivery boy, cultural mediator, interpreter, teacher, political activist, journalist, and bookstore manager.

His debut bestseller, *Io, venditore di elefanti: Una vita per forza fra Dakar, Parigi e Milano* (Milan: Garzanti, 1990), written in collaboration with Oreste Pivetta and based on his early struggles as an undocumented immigrant, represents a landmark in migration literature and has been translated into English by Rebecca Hopkins as *I Was an Elephant Salesman* (Bloomington: Indiana University Press, 2010). He is also the author of *Nonno Dio e gli spiriti danzanti* (Milan: Baldini & Castoldi, 2005) and *Noi italiani neri* (Milan: Baldini & Castoldi, 2010).

Excerpts of his work have been widely anthologized. His poetry has been published in *Ai confini del verso: Poesia della migrazione in italiano,* ed. Mia Lecomte (Milan: Le Lettere, 2006) and translated in *A New Map: The Poetry of Migrant Writers in Italy,* ed. Mia Lecomte and Luigi Bonaffini (Ottawa: Legas, 2011). Now a naturalized Italian citizen, Khouma devotes his efforts to writing and lecturing about the immigrant experience in Italy. His articles have appeared in *Epoca*, *Il Diario*, *l'Unità*, *Linus*, *Metro*, and *Sette*. He is one of the founders and editor-in-chief of the E-zine of migration literature *El Ghibli* and founder and director of *Assaman*, an online magazine of Italian-African information.

Kossi Komla-Ebri was born in 1954 in Tsévié, Togo, and earned his high school diploma in France. In 1974 he moved to Italy where he graduated from the universities of Bologna and Milan with a degree in medicine and specialization in general surgery. He currently lives and practices medicine in the province of Como. As a naturalized Italian citizen, Komla-Ebri plays an active role in local politics to promote the status of migrant workers. In 2001, he became the first African-Italian to run for Parliament.

Komla-Ebri is the author of the novel *Neyla* (Milan: Edizioni dell'Arco, 2002), translated into English by Peter N. Pedroni (Madison, NJ: Fairleigh Dickinson University Press, 2004). His publications include the novel *La sposa degli dei: Nell'Africa degli antichi riti* (Gorle (BG): Marna, 2005), and four collections of short stories and anecdotes: *All'incrocio dei sentieri* (Bologna: EMI, 2003); *Vita e sogni: Racconti in concerto* (Milan: Edizioni dell'Arco, 2007); *Imbarazzismi: quotidiani imbarazzi in bianco e in nero* (Milan: Edizioni dell'Arco, 2002); and *Nuovi imbarazzismi: quotidiani imbarazzi in bianco e in nero e a colori* (Milan: Edizioni dell'Arco, 2004).

His essays and short stories have appeared in magazines and anthologies published in Italy, France, and the United States. Komla-Ebri has won literary awards including first prize for short fiction at the third Eks&Tra competition (1997), as well as a number of awards for his work as cultural mediator, promoting intercultural dialogue and awareness. He is one of the founders as well as a member of the editorial board of the E-zine of migration literature *El Ghibli*. He is also the founder and current president of REDANI (Network of Black African Diaspora in Italy). With the physician Aldo Lo Curto and Brazilian designer Ubiratan Porto, he is the author of *African Illustrated Health Book,* which is distributed in many African villages to promote health care education.

Photo by Rino Bianchi

Gabriella Kuruvilla is a writer, journalist, and painter born in Milan in 1969 to an Italian mother and an Indian father. She obtained a degree in Industrial Design from the Polytechnic University of Milan, and collaborated with a number of newspapers and magazines, including *Il Corriere della Sera*, *Brava Casa*, *Max*, *Anna*, *Cosmopolitan*, and *Marie Claire*. She has a son and lives in Milan, where she now divides her time between her two great passions, painting and writing. Her artwork has been exhibited both in Italy and abroad.

As Viola Chandra, she is the author of the novel *Media chiara e noccioline* (Rome: Derive Approdi, 2001), the children's book *Questa non è una baby-sitter* (Milan: Terre di Mezzo, 2010), and two short story collections: *È la vita, dolcezza* (Milan: Baldini Castoldi Dalai, 2008; Milan: Morellini, 2014), and *Milano, fin qui tutto bene* (Bari: Laterza, 2012).

Since 2014, she has worked for the publisher Morellini as editor of "Città d'autore," a series of volumes which include her short stories and illustrations: *Milano d'autore* (2014), *Roma d'autore* (2015), *Monaco d'autore* (2016), *Bologna d'autore* (2016), *Genova d'autore* (2017), and *Calabria d'autore* (2018). Other short stories have been published in the anthologies *Pecore nere* (Bari: Laterza, 2005), *Lingua Madre Duemilasette,* ed. Daniela Finocchi (Turin: Edizioni SEB27, 2007), and *Smemoranda 2014* (https://www.smemoranda.it/). English translations of her work have appeared in the anthology *Multicultural Literature in Contemporary Italy,* ed. Marie Orton and Graziella Parati (Madison, NJ: Fairleigh Dickinson University Press, 2007), and in *There Is No Map: The New Italian(s)* (September 2016 issue of *Words Without Borders*). She is one of the winners of the third edition of the Lingua Madre Literary Prize (2007).

Amara Lakhous was born in Algiers, Algeria, in 1970, the sixth of nine children of a Berber family. He attended Arabic school, studied French, and graduated with a degree in Philosophy from the University of Algiers. After briefly working as a reporter for Algerian national radio, he fled Algeria's repressive political and cultural climate in 1995 and moved to Rome, where he obtained a degree in Cultural Anthropology from the University La Sapienza and worked as a cultural mediator, interpreter, and translator.

Lakhous wrote his first book in Algerian dialect in 1993. It was published four years later in a bilingual Italian-Arabic edition: *Le cimici e il pirata* (Rome: Arlem, 1999). Inspired by his passion for Italian culture, he began writing in his adopted language, seeking to create a new style that could "Arabicize" Italian and "Italianize" Arabic. His second book, *Scontro di civiltà per un ascensore a Piazza Vittorio* (Rome: Edizioni E/O, 2006) is the re-creation in Italian of another Arabic-language novel based on his early years in Rome, which was released in 2003 in Algeria and Lebanon. The book received critical and popular acclaim, and was made into a film in 2008.

His subsequent publications include the novels *Divorzio all'islamica a viale Marconi* (Rome: Edizioni E/O, 2010), *Contesa per un maialino italianissimo a San Salvario* (Rome: Edizioni E/O, 2013), and *La zingarata della verginella di Via Ormea* (Rome: Edizioni E/O, 2014). Among other awards, Lakhous is the recipient of the prestigious Flaiano Prize (2006) and Algeria's most important literary award, the Prix des libraires Algeriens (2008). His writings have been translated into numerous languages, including English, French, German, and Dutch. Lakhous lived in Italy for eighteen years as a political refugee, an immigrant and, as of 2008, a citizen. He moved to New York in 2014 and has since worked to become a trilingual writer, adding English to the languages that he seeks to mix and "contaminate" through literature.

Tahar Lamri (Algiers, 1958) is an Algerian narrator, performer, and journalist. From 1979 to 1984 he resided in Bengasi, Libya, where he completed his Law degree and worked as translator for the French Consulate. He then moved to France and finally to Ravenna, Italy, where he has lived since 1986, working as a translator and linguistic consultant. Lamri's mother tongue is Sabir, a Mediterranean lingua franca that combines Arabic, Italian, Spanish, French, and other elements. French and Arabic are the languages he learned in school, and Italian is his adopted literary language.

Lamri began writing short stories directly in Italian after settling in Italy. In 1995 he won the prize for narrative in the first edition of the Eks&Tra Award; he then served as jury member in subsequent editions of the contest. His short stories, plays, and essays have appeared in journals such as *El Ghibli*, *Internazionale*, *Kúmá*, and *Sagarana*, and in several anthologies: *Le voci dell'arcobaleno,* ed. Alessandro Ramberti and Roberta Sangiorgi (Santarcangelo di Romagna (RI): Fara Editore, 1995); *Anime in viaggio: La nuova mappa dei popoli* (Rome: Adnkronos, 2001); *Parole di sabbia,* ed. F. Argento, A. Melandri, and P. Trabucco (Mercato San Severino (SA): Edizioni Il Grappolo, 2002); *La seconda pelle,* ed. Roberta Sangiorgi (San Giovanni in Persiceto (BO): Eks&Tra, 2004); *Il carro di pickipò,* ed. P. Gavagna and R. Taddeo (Rome: Ediesse, 2006); and *Mondopentola,* ed. Laila Wadia (Isernia: Cosmo Iannone, 2007).

He is the author of *I sessanta nomi dell'amore* (Santarcangelo di Romagna (RI): Fara Editore, 2006; Naples: Michele Di Salvo Editore, 2007), a collection of short stories (some previously published) framed by the e-mail correspondence/love-story between a Maghrebi man and a young Italian woman. English translations of his work have appeared in *Mediterranean Crossroads,* ed. Graziella Parati (Madison, NJ: Fairleigh Dickinson University Press, 1999); and *Multicultural Literature in Contemporary Italy,* ed. Marie Orton and Graziella Parati (Madison, NJ: Fairleigh Dickinson University Press, 2007). Lamri's artistic activity includes video productions and theatrical performances.

He has collaborated with Teatro delle Albe, a theatrical company based in Ravenna. He is also director of the annual cultural festival sponsored by the city of Ravenna, and editor of the intercultural periodical *Città Meticcia.*

≈

Geneviève Makaping was born in 1958 in Bafoussam, Cameroon. She fled her homeland at the age of sixteen for sentimental reasons, and settled first in France and then in Italy, where she has lived since 1988. She obtained a degree in Modern Foreign Languages and Literatures and a Ph.D. in Multimedia Didactic Technologies and Communication Systems from the University of Calabria, where she also taught Cultural Anthropology.

Makaping is a writer, journalist, and anthropologist. She is the author of the autobiographical essay *Traiettorie di sguardi: E se gli* altri *foste voi?* (Soveria Mannelli (CZ): Rubbettino, 2001), and her columns, essays and short stories have been published in newspapers and periodicals such as *La Provincia Cosentina*, *Il Mulino*, and *Nigrizia*. Her work has also been included in the anthologies *Pace in parole migranti* (Nardò (LE): Besa, 2003), and *Nuovo Planetario Italiano: Geografia e antologia della letteratura della migrazione in Italia e in Europa,* ed. Armando Gnisci (Troina (EN): Città Aperta, 2006).

She was one of the winners of the 2002 edition of the Eks&Tra contest for migrant writers. Makaping directed the newspaper *La Provincia Cosentina*, the first non-Italian woman to hold such a position, and conducted numerous investigative reports on the Calabrian mafia. She is a regular contributor to local radio and television stations. Her career as a journalist earned her the lifetime achievement award from the Mostafà Souhir Prize for Multiculturalism in the Media (2006). She defines herself as a woman with a complex identity — African, Cameroonian, Bamiléké, Italian, and Calabrian. Her work finds inspiration in the multiculturalism and multilingualism of Calabria, the southern Italian region that she has chosen as her second homeland.

≈

Ndjock Ngana (Ilanga, 1952), also known by the Italian name Teodoro, is a Cameroonian–Italian poet and writer. He comes from a family of farmers politically active in the struggle for Cameroon's independence and began writing socially engaged poetry in the early 1970s while attending the university in Yaoundé. He moved to Italy in 1973 and currently lives in Rome, where he works as a cultural mediator and director of the intercultural center Kel'Lam, which he founded in 2000 with the goal of promoting the integration of immigrants.

Ngana published two volumes of poetry in Bàsàá (his native language) and Italian: *Ñhindô / Nero* (Rome: Anterem, 1994; Rome: Kel'Lam, 1999); and *Il segreto della capanna / Djimb li lapga* (Rome: Lilith, 1998). Other publications include collections of poems and short stories: *Foglie vive calpestate: Riflessioni sotto il Baobab* (Rome: UCSEI, 1989); *Stress 1: Quel maledetto pezzo di carta!* (Rome: Kel'Lam, 2004); *Màébà. Dialoghi con mia figlia* (Rome: Kel'Lam, 2005); and *βàà Lóñ Afrîkà? / La Nostra Africa* (Rome: VIS, 2017). He has also written a children's book for "young polyglots," *Dingangana* (Rome: Kel'Lam, 2009): a collection of stories from the Bàsàá tradition in four versions (Bàsàá, Italian, Romanian, and Albanian).

His poems have appeared in the anthologies *Nuovo Planetario Italiano: Geografia e antologia della letteratura della migrazione in Italia e in Europa,* ed. Armando Gnisci (Troina (EN): Città Aperta, 2006), and *Ai confini del verso: Poesia della migrazione in italiano,* ed. Mia Lecomte (Milan: Le Lettere, 2006). A selection of his poems has been translated into English in *A New Map: The Poetry of Migrant Writers in Italy,* ed. Mia Lecomte and Luigi Bonaffini (Ottawa: Legas, 2011).

Jarmila Očkayová was born in Slovakia in 1955. She moved to Italy in 1974 and graduated from the University of Bologna. Now an Italian citizen, she lives in Reggio Emilia where she works as a translator. She began writing when she was very young and published poems and short stories in periodicals in Bratislava.

Her move to Italy resulted in a ten-year creative break brought about by the change to a new writing language followed by the publication of her debut novel in Italian, *Verrà la vita e avrà i tuoi occhi* (Milan: Baldini Castoldi Dalai, 1995), and by several other novels: *L'essenziale è invisibile agli occhi* (Milan: Baldini Castoldi Dalai, 1997); *Requiem per tre padri* (Milan: Baldini Castoldi Dalai, 1998); *Appuntamento nel bosco* (San Dorligo della Valle (TS): Edizioni EL, 1998); and *Occhio a Pinocchio* (Isernia: Cosmo Iannone, 2006), which won the Popoli in cammino Prize.

Other publications include her translation of a collection of Slovak folktales originally edited by Pavol Dobšinký, *Il re del tempo e altre fiabe slovacche* (Palermo: Sellerio, 1988). Her work has been anthologized in the following volumes: *Nuovo Planetario Italiano: Geografia e antologia della letteratura della migrazione in Italia e in Europa*, ed. Armando Gnisci (Troina (EN): Città Aperta, 2006); *San Nicola: Agiografia immaginaria,* ed. M. Lobaccaro and R. Kubati (Molfetta (BA): La meridiana, 2006); and *Alfabetica 2007* (Iesi (AN): Edizioni Gei, 2007).

Candelaria Romero was born in 1973 in San Miguel de Tucuman, Argentina, to poet parents. When she was three, her family fled to Bolivia in order to escape Argentina's dictatorship, and then to Sweden (1979), where they obtained political asylum and where Romero later acquired Swedish nationality. In 1991 she graduated from the School of Drama Arts Södra Latin of Stockholm and went on to study theater and dance in Denmark, Spain, and Italy. She has lived in Bergamo, Italy, since 1992, working as an actress, writer, and theater producer.

Romero is the author of a collection of plays, *Poetica e teatro civile* (Rome: Aracne, 2010), and two poetry collections: *Poesie di fine mondo* (Faloppio (CO): LietoColle, 2010), and *Salto mortale* (Faloppio (CO): LietoColle, 2014). Her work has been published in *Lingua Madre Duemilanove: Racconti di donne straniere in Italia,* ed. Daniela Finocchi (Turin: Edizioni SEB27, 2009), and in the journals *Caffè*, *El Ghibli*, *Kúmá,* and *Sagarana.* A selection of her poems has been included in the anthology *Ai confini del verso: Poesia della migrazione in italiano,* ed. Mia Lecomte (Milan: Le Lettere, 2006), and translated into English in *A New Map: The Poetry of Migrant Writers in Italy,* ed. Mia Lecomte and Luigi Bonaffini (Ottawa: Legas, 2011).

Romero is the co-founder of the E-zine of migration literature *El Ghibli.* She is a member of Compagnia delle poete and has worked with other theater companies, staging plays and poetry performances throughout Italy. She also designs and delivers narrative, theater, and poetry workshops and is active as an intercultural educator, collaborating with numerous local, national, and international organizations. Her recognitions include the National Prize Bianca Maria Pirazzoli for Best Actress (2008).

Barbara Serdakowski was born in Poland (Gryfino, 1964). As a result of her father's work, she grew up in Morocco, and later emigrated to Canada (1974), where she acquired Canadian nationality and graduated from Concordia University in Montreal. After marrying Italian artist Cesare Oliva, she first moved to Venezuela, and then to Florence, Italy, where she has lived since 1996.

Serdakowski began her literary career writing in French. She subsequently adopted Italian as a language of literary expression, and she has written multilingual poetry combining all the languages of her migrant cultural background. She has published two novels, *Katerina e la sua guerra* (Turin: Robin Edizioni, 2009) and *Gli aranci di Tadeusz* (Rome: Ensemble, 2018), and three poetry anthologies: *La verticalità di esistere linearmente* (Florence: L'Autore Libri, 2010), *Così nuda* (Rome: Ensemble, 2012), and *Senza verbo* (Faloppio (CO): LietoColle, 2017).

Her short stories and poems have been published in numerous Italian and international periodicals and several anthologies, including: *Anime in viaggio* (Rome: Adnkronos, 2001), *Kaboom* (Massa: Edizioni Clandestine, 2002); *Impronte: Scritture dal mondo* (Nardò (LE): Besa, 2003); *Ai confini del verso: Poesia della migrazione in italiano,* ed. Mia Lecomte (Milan: Le Lettere, 2006); *Nuovo Planetario Italiano: Geografia e antologia della letteratura della migrazione in Italia e in Europa,* ed. Armando Gnisci (Troina (EN): Città Aperta, 2006); and *San Nicola: Agiografia immaginaria,* ed. M. Lobaccaro and R. Kubati (Molfetta (BA): La meridiana, 2006).

English translations of her work are anthologized in *Multicultural Literature in Contemporary Italy,* ed. Marie Orton and Graziella Parati (Madison, NJ: Fairleigh Dickinson University Press, 2007), and *A New Map: The Poetry of Migrant Writers in Italy,* ed. Mia Lecomte and Luigi Bonaffini (Ottawa: Legas, 2011). Serdakowski is co-founder of the Centro d'Arte e Ricerca Magma in Florence and a member of Compagnia delle poete. She has won several literary prizes, including an award for short fiction in the sixth edition of the Eks&Tra contest.

Laila Wadia was born in India (Mumbai, 1966) and moved to Italy in 1986. She is a resident of Trieste, where she works as an English teacher at the University of Trieste. She also works as travel and social affairs journalist for numerous Italian magazines and newspapers.

A self-described "storyteller," Wadia has published two collections of short stories, *Il burattinaio e altre storie extra-italiane* (Isernia: Cosmo Iannone, 2004) and *Se tutte le donne* (Siena: Barbera, 2012), and three novels: *Amiche per la pelle* (Rome: Edizioni E/O, 2007); *Come diventare italiani in 24 ore* (Florence: Barbera, 2010); and *Algoritmi indiani* (Trieste: Vita Activa Edizioni, 2017). Her publications also include a translingual book of erotic food poetry, *Kitchensutra* (Amazon KDP, 2016), and the biography *Il testimone di Pirano* (Formigine (MO): Infinito Edizioni, 2016).

Her short stories and poems have appeared in journals such as *El Ghibli*, *La rivista dell'Arte*, *Kúmá*, and *Sagarana*, and in numerous anthologies, including: *La seconda pelle,* ed. Roberta Sangiorgi (San Giovanni in Persiceto (BO): Eks&Tra, 2004); *Pecore nere* (Bari: Laterza, 2005); *San Nicola: Agiografia immaginaria,* ed. M. Lobaccaro and R. Kubati (Molfetta (BA): La meridiana, 2006); *Il carro di pickipò,* ed. P. Gavagna and R. Taddeo (Rome: Ediesse, 2006); *Mondopentola* (Isernia: Cosmo Iannone, 2007), which she also edited; and *Roba da donne: Emancipazione e scrittura nei percorsi di autrici dal mondo,* ed. Silvia Camilotti (Rome: Mangrovie Edizioni, 2009).

English translations of her work have been published in *Metamorphoses* (Spring and Fall 2006), *Multicultural Literature in Contemporary Italy,* ed. Marie Orton and Graziella Parati (Madison, NJ: Fairleigh Dickinson University Press, 2007), *The AALITRA Review* 8 (2014), and *There Is No Map: The New Italian(s)* (September 2016 issue of *Words Without Borders*). Wadia has turned several of her stories into plays, including *Amiche per la pelle*, which has also been adapted for the screen as *Babylon Sisters* (2017). Among other recognitions, she was awarded first place for short fiction in the 2004 Eks&Tra contest, the Italian President's Medal for Literary Contribution (2004), and first place in the Popoli in cammino Prize (2006).

Yousef Wakkas was born in Azaz, Syria in 1955 and immigrated to Italy in 1982. He began writing in 1995, while serving a prison sentence, and achieved numerous recognitions for his short fiction, including first prize in the 1996 and 1998 editions of the Eks&Tra contest, and the Italian President's Medal for Literary Contribution (1998). In 2005 he was repatriated to Syria, where he worked as a translator and contributed to Arabic-language literary periodicals. He currently lives in Milan, having been forced to flee his home country in Septemeber 2015 due to the on-going Syrian conflict.

Wakkas is the author of three novels: *L'uomo parlante* (Milan: Edizioni dell'Arco, 2006); *Opera 99: L'autobus dei sogni* (Youcanprint, 2016); and *Sulla via di Berlino: La marcia* (Isernia: Cosmo Iannone, 2017). He has also published three volumes of short stories: *Fogli sbarrati: Viaggio reale e surreale tra immigrati e carcerati* (San Giovanni in Persiceto (BO): Eks&Tra, 2001); *Terra mobile* (Isernia: Cosmo Iannone, 2004); and *La talpa nel soffitto* (Milan: Edizioni dell'Arco, 2005).

His work has appeared in numerous anthologies, including: *Le voci dell'arcobaleno,* ed. Alessandro Ramberti and Roberta Sangiorgi (Santarcangelo di Romagna (RI): Fara Editore, 1995); *Mosaici d'inchiostro,* ed. Roberta Sangiorgi (Santarcangelo di Romagna (RI): Fara Editore, 1996); *Memorie in valigia,* ed. Alessandro Ramberti and Roberta Sangiorgi (Santarcangelo di Romagna (RI): Fara Editore, 1997); *Destini sospesi di volti in cammino,* ed. Alessandro Ramberti and Roberta Sangiorgi (Santarcangelo di Romagna (RI): Fara Editore, 1998); *Italiani per vocazione,* ed. Igiaba Scego (Fiesole: Cadmo, 2005); *San Nicola: Agiografia immaginaria,* ed. M. Lobaccaro and R. Kubati (Molfetta (BA): La meridiana, 2006); *Mondopentola,* ed. Laila Wadia (Isernia: Cosmo Iannone, 2007); and *Pubblichiamoli a casa loro: Prove letterarie di umorismo migrante,* ed. Matteo Andreone and Raffaele Taddeo (Rome: Ensemble, 2018).

English translations of his work have appeared in *Mediterranean Crossroads,* ed. Graziella Parati (Madison, NJ: Fairleigh Dickinson

University Press, 1999) and *Multicultural Literature in Contemporary Italy*, ed. Marie Orton and Graziella Parati (Madison, NJ: Fairleigh Dickinson University Press, 2007).

This Book Was Completed on 29 October 2019

At Italica Press in Bristol UK.

It Was Set in Garamond,

Garamond Expert

& Wingdings.

www.ingramcontent.com/pod-product-compliance
Ingram Content Group UK Ltd.
Pitfield, Milton Keynes, MK11 3LW, UK
UKHW041842190726
13854UKWH00002B/664